School of Hard Knocks

Sandra Wynn

Vineyard Place
2017

Copyright © 2017 by Sandra Wynn

All rights reserved. No part of this book may be reproduced or transmitted in any form or by any means, electronic or mechanical, including photocopying, recording or by any information storage and retrieval system, except for brief quotations within a review, without permission in writing from the author.

Contact Sandra Wynn at sandrawynn1939@gmail.com

Published by Create Space.

Printed in the United States of America

ISBN 978-1978380479

Edition: edit 1

Dedication

This book is dedicated to my husband Wayne. He was a quiet man, and his life spoke volumes in the way that he lived. He loved me with tenderness, a love that was gentle and dedicated. He lives in my heart and soul.
I love you, Wayne,

Your wife, Sandra

Table of Contents

Chapter 1	7
Chapter 2	12
Chapter 3	16
Chapter 4	26
Chapter 5	35
Chapter 6	38
Chapter 7	44
Chapter 8	49
Chapter 9	57
Chapter 10	70
Chapter 11	73
Chapter 12	77
Chapter 13	80
Chapter 14	86
Chapter 15	104
Chapter 16	109
Chapter 17	118
Chapter 18	130
Chapter 19	152
Chapter 20	157

1

It was December 31, 1955, in Denver, Colorado. My friend, Cindy, wanted to go roller skating at the local rink; I didn't want to go - I wanted to go to the movies.

"Oh, come on," she begged. "My boyfriend, Wally, is bringing a friend with him and I want you to meet him. You'll like him."

"How do you know I will like him?" I asked.

"Because he is good-looking, charming, personality plus, and he's in the Army."

"So, what's the big deal about that?" I wanted to know.

"No big deal, but I know you like service guys, because you go out with Air Force boys."

"That's different," I said. "I pick them out myself. I don't want you picking a guy out for me."

"I am not picking out anyone for you. I just want you to meet him."

"So, how long have you known about this?"

"Since last weekend," Cindy replied.

"Why did you wait a whole week to ask me about going skating tonight?"

"I knew you would argue with me about it, and I was right."

"How have you got this whole thing set up?" I wanted to know.

"We are supposed to meet them at the rink at eight."

"How are we getting home after skating?"

"They have a car, so they will take us home."

"Okay," I said, "but this is the first and last time I am going to do anything like this again."

Cindy and I arrived at the rink at seven-thirty. We put on our skates, and out to the floor we went. The place was packed with people wearing hats and blowing horns, getting ready for the New Year. Cindy elbowed me as we made our way around the rink. "There they are, standing over there by the rail!"

"Boy, is he ever good looking!" I said to myself. *Where did Wally find such a nice-looking friend? After all, Wally is kind of dumpy looking, not much to look at, if you know what I mean.*

We rolled over to the rail to talk to the boys. Wally said, "Sandra, this is Bob. Bob, this is Sandra." Bob reached out and took my hand in his.

"I am so pleased to meet you," he said.

My fingers tingled as he held my hand - my pulse beat faster and my legs felt like mush. As I stared into his brown eyes which were the color of warm honey, the only thing I could manage to say was, "Me too."

I had butterflies in my stomach as he said, "Can I skate with you?"

"Oh, of course, please do," I replied.

We skated to the music the organ played, songs like "Let Me Call You Sweetheart" (I'm in love with you), and "When You are in Love" (it's the loveliest night of the year). I was in dreamland and skating on air. It was midnight before I knew it. The horns were blowing, people were shouting "Happy New Year!" and kissing each other. Bob took me in his arms and gave me the sweetest kiss I have ever had.

It was time to make the trip home. While we were taking off our skates and putting on our shoes, Bob asked me if he could see me again. "Wally and I, we only get a weekend pass twice-a-month."

"I would be delighted to go out with you again."

As we rode along in the car, Wally and Cindy in the front seat and Bob and I in the back, I asked, "Where are you and Wally stationed?"

"In Vail, Colorado," he replied.

It was one a.m. before we parted. I went in the apartment where I lived with Mom and Dad. Bob went on his way back to base with Wally.

Monday morning came, and it was time to think about school. Cindy and I hadn't attended since the middle of November. I gathered my books as usual, and got ready to go. I walked the six blocks to get Cindy. She answered the door when I knocked, picked up her books and we were on our way. This was another day of no school; we went to Eva's house.

Eva was ten years older than we were. We were sixteen-going-on-thirty. She was married, her husband's name was Jim. He was quiet, gentle and kind. He went to work every day with no complaints. They had a beautiful daughter named Annie. Annie was three, brown curly hair the color of chestnuts, warm brown eyes, and a dimple on each check. She was sweet and kind like her daddy.

Many times, Annie was left to be on her own. When Cindy and I were there, we took care of her, made sure she had breakfast and clean clothes to put on.

Eva was the neighborhood prostitute. There was always beer in the frig. She was always glad to see us because that meant we would take care of Annie while she entertained her male friends.

It was Monday afternoon - we were playing cards with Eva, and Annie was taking a nap. There was a loud knock at the door. "Open the door, Eva! I know Cindy is in there!" yelled Cindy's mother, Rose

Before Eva could open the door, Rose had already barged into the room. She had short brown hair, brittle-like-straw, bristling blue eyes, and a high-pitched voice when she was angry. She was boiling mad. "You girls have not been to school in three weeks!"

"Oh," I said. "we haven't been there since the middle of November."

"What are you going to do about it?" she asked.

"Nothing." I replied. "I am going to quit school and get married."

"Just who are you going to marry?" she wanted to know.

"I can't tell you, I don't know yet, it's a secret."

"I've had enough of you, Sandra. You're not a good influence on my daughter. If you two were not friends, my daughter would still be in school!"

"Wait just a minute, Rose. Are you saying that your daughter can't think for herself? I haven't loaned her any of my brain cells to think with."

"YOU wait just a minute, Mother - Sandra's my friend. If I wanted to go to school, I would have been there. School is boring; I want to quit and get a job."

"No point in talking about this anymore. I can see you two girls have all the answers."

Rose was beside herself with anger. Her face was red, her eyes the size of quarters, and close to tears. As she walked to the door, she turned to face Cindy, tears flowing down her cheeks. Her voice cracked: "Cindy, I love you dearly. I just want what is best for you and Sandra. I will see you at home."

"Why did you tell my mother you were going to get married?"

"That was the first thing that popped into my head."

"Good thinking there, Sandra. She will be griping about that for weeks."

"Maybe you can calm her down."

"Fat chance of that. I will just stay gone."

"It's time for me to go home and see what's going on at my house."

"Are you going to tell your mom that you want to quit school?"

"No, I'm just going to do it, and she will find out later. I'm going to go and turn in my books tomorrow. Do you want to meet me at school?"

"Sure," she replied.

I saw Buford walking toward me; in my mind, he was an old man. He was in his late sixties, a retired steam and electrical engineer. He had a receding hair line, was short and overweight, and had a large stomach, with steel gray eyes that could look a hole right through you, if he thought you were telling him a lie. Buford was the owner of the apartment building we were moving to. I had talked to him about the apartment a few weeks ago. "Hi, Sandra! The apartment is ready for you, your mom and sisters to move into."

"That's wonderful! We can start moving this

weekend," I replied. "There's one problem I want to take care of before this weekend. We have a record player that my mother doesn't want to give to my dad. Can I bring it over tomorrow evening? Will you be home?'

"I'll be home all evening; you can come anytime."

"Thank you, Buford. I'll see you tomorrow."

When I got home, mother was pacing the floor, wringing her hands and talking to herself in a loud voice. "That no good, rotten son-of-a-bitch, wants to take the record player!"

"Calm down, Mother. I've already taken care of the problem. I talked to Buford on my way home. The player will be moved tomorrow night."

"Your dad will be mad when he comes over and sees the player is gone."

"So what? He's always mad about something. I'll take care of him."

Here I am, trying to figure out how we are going to move. The only thing Mom and Dad are concerned about, is who is going to get the player? They are finally going to get a divorce - they have fought with each other for as long as I can remember. I have never heard them say a kind word to each other. They must have loved each other at some point in time. I wonder what happened that tore them apart? I can't be concerned about this stuff now; I need to get Janice and her two friends, Dennis and David, to help us move.

2

Janice was my younger sister. She had long, blond hair which she kept braided, wore jeans and a T-shirt, always wore a hat and cowboy boots. She was the neighborhood mechanic. If you had a problem with your bike, Janice could fix it. She was good at playing marbles and football. Bike parts were kept under her bed, and nuts and bolts were kept in a cigar box. The marbles she had won, were kept in an oatmeal box.

Karen was the baby. She was four years younger than I was. She was thin, fragile and frail looking. She had short blond hair, blue eyes, and thin legs and arms. We used to call her 'spaghetti legs'.

Janice and I went over to see if David and Dennis would help us move on Saturday. They were twin boys the same age as Janice, fourteen. David had brown hair and blue eyes. Dennis was blond and brown-eyed. David was easy going and gentle, his brother was hot-headed and bossy. Of course, I was the big

The following day, I met Cindy at school, and we turned in our books. Quitting wasn't difficult as nobody asked us any questions. We were out of there in ten minutes.

David and Dennis came over the next afternoon to move the player. We thought we could put it in the wagon and wheel it the two blocks. It was too large, too wide, and too long. "Now what are we going to do?" I wanted to know.

"We can carry it," Janice replied.

Dennis said, "I'll take the bottom, my brother can take the top, and you and Janice can take the sides."

"You know this player is going to be heavy carrying up the street," I replied.

David turned and looked at me. "That's okay. We can stop and rest."

"Okay," I said. "Let's get going."

I knocked on the door. Buford let us in and

unlocked the door to the apartment. We placed the player in the corner of the room, plugged it in and turned it on. It still worked. "Would you mind if we moved the records tonight?"

"Tell you what - I'll leave the doors unlocked, and when you are finished, knock on my door so I can lock the place up."

"That's a deal," I replied.

We moved all the records in three trips with the wagon. When we finally get moved into our new place, we'll have things that we have never had before - a bedroom, bathroom, and a refrigerator. We will really be living - we can have ice cubes in our glass of water!

"Sandra, how come you are not ready to go to school?" Mother asked.

"I don't have any school until Monday; it's the teachers' workshop. I am going to get some packing done. I can pack some of the stuff we are not using. The items in the pantry, linens we are not using, and some of our clothes. Saturday will be here before you know it, and I want some of this stuff packed up and ready to go. We can take the boxes over and unpack them, and then bring them back and refill them. Safeway had only six boxes, and won't have any more until next week."

"Hey, Sandra, here comes the Old Man!" Janice said. "I'm going to get out of here. I will be under the porch; just let me know when he's gone."

"Okay," I replied.

None of us ever called him Dad; he was always the 'Old Man'.

"Where in the hell is the record player?" he yelled.

"I moved it," I replied.

"What the hell do you mean, you moved it? You had no business moving the record player!"

"Oh, yes I did! That player is Mother's. There are four of us, and only one of you. If you want to listen to records, buy a player of your own."

"Where are the records?"

"With the player."

"I'll fix this! I am going over to Buford's right now. I'll get the player and the records."

"No, you won't! Buford will call the police and have you removed as a trespasser. I have already talked to him about the situation."

"You little bitch! You are enough to drive Jesus Christ off the cross!"

"You're walking on thin ice. I know a lot of stuff about you, things that would make you look pretty bad."

He knew I had won. He slammed the door on his way out. I'm glad mother was not here. This way, he couldn't drag her into the argument.

I went out to tell Janice that the Old Man was gone. She was already coming out of her hiding place. "Why did you tell him that Buford would call the police?"

"First of all, he doesn't have any business going over to Buford's, and second of all, it worked. "Tomorrow is moving day. Janice, what time are David and Dennis coming?"

"They will be here at ten," she replied.

They arrived at ten. I had all the plates packed. I placed newspaper in between each one so they would not get broken. "Okay, you guys, all of the plates are in this box. It's real heavy, so I suggest we place it in the wagon. We will have to lift the wagon up and down the curbs," I said.

Dennis does not like the idea that we are only take one box. I call him 'Mr. Hot Head'. "If we are going to take just one box at a time this whole trip, we are going to be doing this all weekend!" Dennis yelled. "Do you have a better idea?" I wanted to know.

"Well no," he replied.

"That's just like a fourteen-year-old," I said. "So, get your butt busy so we can get this show on the road."

"Okay, Miss Boss Bucket," he replied.

"Now listen here, Mr. Dennis. This is the only trip we will be taking one box. Do you have that square in your mind, or do I have to draw you a picture?" I shouted.

"Yes, I got it," he said.

"Here is the deal: when we get to the apartment, you guys are going to place the box on the kitchen table. I am going to put the plates in the cupboard. While I am doing that, you guys can go back and load up the other boxes - they are all packed. And wake up Karen. It's about time for her to be up anyway," I said.

Janice wanted to know if there was anything else they should do. "Yes, there is. When you get back, take this large box with you and put your repair stuff in it, as well as your nuts and bolts and oatmeal box that has your marbles in it. I don't want those items stored under the bed," I replied.

"Just where am I going to put my stuff?" she wanted to know.

"We have a back porch now, that we have never had before, so we can put those bike tires out there. The rest of the items can go on a shelf in the pantry. We have more space to put things," I said quietly.

They were back in and had Karen with them, and all the rest of the boxes. "Where do you want the rest of the boxes?" David wanted to know.

"Bring the boxes with the dishes, and put them on the table; the rest of the boxes you can put on the bed. While you guys are gone with the large box loading up Janice's repair stuff, Karen and I will unload the rest of these boxes," I replied.

They returned with Janice's tools and clothes piled on top of the box. How much is left?" I wanted to know.

"Not much - a few pots and pans, some clothes, and shoes," Janice replied.

"How about if we leave the rest of it until Monday? We have done enough work for the weekend. It will take us a while to get this stuff put away. Let's go get Mother. She can stay here with us," I said.

3

When we got back to the old apartment, Mother was just finishing her breakfast of toast and coffee. She was still in her nightclothes. "Where have you kids been?" Mother asked.

"We have been moving the stuff over to the other apartment. You were sleeping like a dead person. We were afraid we were going to wake you up, since we were making a lot of racket. I kept telling David and Dennis to be quiet," Janice replied.

"We have moved almost everything. Come on, Mother - we will show you there is not much left. There is nothing left in the pantry, all of the dishes are gone, and we left your cup and small plate on the table so you could put your toast on it. The pots and pans are gone, linens, and most of the clothes. We left some clothes for you to put on so there is no reason to stay here for the weekend. Come on Janice, let's help Mother get her stuff together. We will get the rest of the items on Monday," I ordered.

I thought Mother might put up a fuss, but she didn't. I hope the new place will help mother to calm down. I sure hope Mother does better over here. She never makes any decisions. If she thinks she has to solve a problem of some kind, she has a fit. It goes like this: "I don't know what to do", "I can't fix anything, you will have to do it yourself." We learned very early to solve our own problems. When a situation comes up mother does not want to do, I am always afraid she will do what she did a few years ago.

I will never forget this: I was awakened from a sound sleep, to yelling and screaming in the kitchen. The Old Man is screaming at Mother, "Shut your mouth and go to bed! There is nothing around your neck and the walls are not moving!" he ordered. I hear Mother yelling: "There are chains around my neck, they're strangling me, the walls are moving, they're going to suffocate me! Do something! I am going to die if you don't!"

I was terrified and bolted out of bed. I knew I had

to do something. The Old Man's eyes were bulging, his face was red, and he was pounding his fist on the table. Mother's eyes were glassy, she looked wild, she was scared, and looked like a trapped animal. I ran into the kitchen and looked from one to the other, the old man screaming and Mother yelling! I yelled, "Stop! What is going on in here?"

"She's just having a fit," the old man replied.

"What do you mean, she's just having a fit?" I wanted to know. "You get your butt to bed and I will take care of Mother!" I yelled at the Old Man

I went over to the pantry and got a washcloth, walked over to the sink, put cold water on the cloth, placed it on Mother's forehead, and began to rub her neck. I began to talk softly to her: "It's okay, Mother, I am here now and I will take good care of you. The walls have stopped moving, and the chains are gone."

She began to relax, her breathing slowed down, and she started looking sleepy. "Mother," I said, "it's time to go to bed."

"Okay," she replied. Then she got up and went to bed. I will never forget it, and it has never been talked about.

"Come on, are you about ready to go?" I asked. "I'm getting hungry for lunch. By the way, what are we going to eat?

"I'm sure we will find something," Janice replied.

"Sandra, how did you find this apartment?" Mother wanted to know.

"I was talking to Buford a few weeks ago; he said he had an apartment that would be available in a few weeks. I asked him if he would be willing to rent to us. He said he would be delighted to have us as renters."

"I hope you didn't tell him about our problems. I don't want you airing our dirty laundry in public for the whole world to know what's going on."

"Now why in the world would I tell Buford our trash? First of all, he is not the kind of person I would share any information about my personal life. Buford is just Buford - he had something we needed and that is all there is to it. If you decide you want to fuss about what Buford knows or doesn't know, go right ahead."

"The living room would look a lot better if it was a different color. Lime-green just does not do a thing for me. Besides that, Bob and I have been talking about getting married."

Mother screamed, "What about school?"

"I quit school," I replied.

"What do you mean, you quit school? Now what are you going to do?"

"I'm going to get married and live happily ever after," I replied. "Now look Mother, you and Dad are getting divorced and I will be one less kid for you to worry about."

"What is your dad going to say about all of this?"

"Probably nothing. He won't have to pay any child support for me. Besides that, what could he do about it anyway? The most he could do is have a temper tantrum, and he is always having those. So, what's the big deal?"

"You have got it all figured out, just get married and live happily ever after. Well, good luck. There is nothing I can say to change your mind."

"Thank you, Mother, there is nothing you could say to change my mind. Now that we have that settled, I am going to go and see if Buford has any paint."

"Just what color are you planning to paint the living room?" Janice wanted to know.

"I was thinking about a cream color or a beige, just depends on what color Buford has," I replied.

"You better ask Buford for some spackle and sandpaper."

"Why do we need spackle and sandpaper?"

"There are always small holes where people have hung pictures, calendars or paintings. The spackle is used to fill in the holes, and the sandpaper is used to smooth it off. "I'm going to paint - I don't want to waste time filling in holes."

"How about this idea? You can do the painting

and I will fix the holes," Janice replied.

"That sounds like a good idea to me. Okay, Janice. The only color Buford had was beige and off-white, so I brought both colors. I thought it would look real nice if the ceiling was off-white and the walls were beige."

"Here's the deal, Sandra. If we are going to paint the ceiling off-white, I will paint it, because you have to have a straight line where the ceiling meets the wall."

"Sounds good to me," I replied.

In the weeks that followed, Janice and I got the living room painted. Janice did a gorgeous job filling in the holes, painting the ceiling, and getting the lines straight; I painted the walls. The entire room looked as if a professional painter had done the painting. We felt like we were living in luxury with a newly painted living room, a refrigerator, and a bedroom we have never had before. And now we could have ice cubes! We were really living!

Bob and I decided to get married on the 16th of May, 1956. His mom and stepdad were making plans to fly to Denver from Portland, Oregon.

Our friend, Eva, became a widow, and her daughter, Annie, lost her Dad to a heart attack. Her husband's income was gone, and Eva could no longer live in the apartment they were renting. Eva and Annie moved to the upstairs apartment in our building.

The male traffic was heavy and steady to Eva's apartment. Annie was a steady visitor to our apartment. I began to tell Annie at night, before she went back upstairs to her apartment, to come back downstairs in the morning. Annie was only four at the time, and seemed to be way beyond her years in wisdom. I decided it was our job to look after Annie; Janice, Karen and I watched over her. Eva didn't seem to miss her husband, but her daughter missed her daddy and wished he would come back.

It was a warm Tuesday morning in April. Annie and I we were eating our breakfast cereal. She looked at me with her serious brown eyes and sweet smile, placed her small hands on her hips, and wanted to know, "Why does my mother have so much company?"

As I sat in my chair next to her, and studied her small face with her innocent brown eyes, how could I tell her that her mother was a prostitute? However, that was a nice word for her, as she was really the neighborhood whore.

I swallowed hard, cleared my throat, and felt tears in my eyes as I replied, "I don't know, Annie. Would you like to go to the park with me today?"

"Oh, yes, can we? I like the park. Can I play on the swings, slide down the slide, and play on the teeter-totter?" she wanted to know.

"Of course you can, and as soon as we finish our breakfast, we will get ready to go. "Now remember, Annie, you will have to walk twelve blocks to the park and back again to get home. Can you make it that far?"

"Oh yes," said Annie. "My legs are strong, and I AM four-years-old, you know!"

I wonder what is going to happen to this precious little girl? She deserves a better life than what she is getting from her mother. I will look after her for as long as I am here. I know I will worry about her after I get married to Bob and move away.

"Come on Annie, are you ready to go?"

"Yes, I am ready," Annie replied.

"What a beautiful day!" I said to myself. "No clouds, blue sky, soft breeze, and not real hot. The temperature is just right. Kind of odd for April, so just enjoy the day and the weather. I can remember times when we have had snow in April. However, I don't think it will snow today."

"Can I play in the sandbox?" Annie wanted to know.

"Of course, you can," I replied. "Are you getting tired, Annie? We have walked ten blocks and have two more blocks to go, plus we have a way to walk before we get to the playground."

"I'm okay," Annie replied.

"Be sure to let me know if you get tired, and I will carry you the rest of the way."

"I can make it - I'm a big girl. I AM four-years-old, you know! Oh, look! There is a sandbox and a lot of kids for me to play with. I just know I'm going to have fun today!"

"Go play in the sand, and I will swing on the swings, and both of us will have fun."

"Okay," Annie replied.

I wonder what kind of life Bob and I will have together? He seems so wonderful at times, and other times he seems to be so sarcastic. He talks very little about his mother and dad. The only thing he has really said is that both of them have been married four times, and each of them are on their fifth marriage. He did tell me his mother left him and his brother when he was three, and his brother was two. She joined the army, and their dad was in the hospital with a broken back. He did not give any details. The neighbors discovered they were alone, because Bob was stealing milk off their porch. The police were called, and they were put in foster care until their dad could care for them. Bob's brother's name was Jim; they had four stepmothers and four stepdads. Sometimes he says thing that are kind of odd, like, "I don't know how to love anybody." Maybe I can teach him.

"Oh-oh, Annie, we better head for home. I see some black clouds and it looks like it could rain."

"I don't want to go right now. I am having too much fun." Her brown eyes filled with tears and she began to sob. "Why do we have to go?"

"We have been here for two hours. You have played on the swings, the slide, the merry-go-round, the teeter-totter, and in the sandbox. I didn't bring a jacket and neither did you, and I don't want us to get wet. It will take a while to get home before it starts to rain."

"Okay," she replied, "but I'm not happy."

"I know, your mother will not be happy if I bring you home and you are soaking wet, because we stayed and played until it started to rain."

"We have made it home, Annie, without getting wet, and here comes the rain."

"Just where in the hell have you been with my

daughter?" yelled Eva.

"Wait just a minute! I left a note on your door hours ago, letting you know I was taking Annie to the park!" I screamed back at Eva."

"I did not find any kind of a note," replied Eva.

"Come along with me, and I will show you where I taped the note to your door." Up the stairs we went, and would you believe, there was the note right where I left it. Did I feel smug? Of course, I did. I turned to Eva and said, "If you would open your eyes and look before you engage your mouth." Then I lowered my voice to almost a whisper and said: "If you payed more attention to little Annie, and less attention to your male traffic and your drinking, you would know what is going on, and I would not have to leave you a note telling you where Annie and I have gone." She gave me a nasty look as she entered her apartment with Annie by her side.

May 1st, fifteen more days and I will be married. We will be happy, life will be wonderful. We will love each other forever.

Maynard and Susie, Bob's mother and stepdad, flew in from Portland, Oregon, to Denver, Colorado, two days before the wedding. They stayed in a hotel a few blocks away from where we lived. The day before the wedding, Bob came to the apartment to let me know he was going to the tavern with his parents.

"I'll come and pick you up in a couple of hours and we'll go out to eat with my folks."

"It's two right now. I will look for you at four-thirty. Is that okay with you?" I wanted to know.

"Yes," he said with a smile, "we should be done by that time."

Four-thirty came and went, five-thirty, six-thirty, and at seven he shows up. I'm upset. "I decided that we were not going to have dinner with your folks, so I made myself a tuna-fish sandwich." I tried to keep my voice calm, as my eyes filled with tears.

Bob placed his arm around my shoulder, "I'm really sorry. My mother got a little drunk."

"Oh, wonderful! Does she often drink too much?" I knew the second that question came out of my mouth that it was the wrong thing to ask.

He dropped his arm from my shoulder, turned me to face him. His eyes were as cold as ice cubes, his voice was stern. "That is none of your business."

"I'm sorry I asked you that question," I said in a small voice.

"Come on Sandra, let's go to the movies. My mother will be okay in the morning."

"Sure, that sounds like fun."

I knew deep inside of me that getting married the next day was going to be something I would regret. What you know inside and what you say outside are two very different things.

May 16th, 1956, two o'clock in the afternoon at Calvary Baptist Church in Denver, Colorado, I became Mrs. Robert Rinebold. I had no idea how I had changed my life within twenty minutes.

I don't know how I felt; it seemed things and events went by on a slow-moving screen. The ceremony was over, it was time to go home, open the wedding gifts, eat cake and drink coffee. We opened the gifts: pots and pans, dishes, silverware, towels, sheets, pillowcases, and bathroom items.

Bob decided to go upstairs and visit with Eva. I wondered what the big attraction was. I knew I would be better off to stay quiet. He looked at me with a small grin. "I won't stay very long," and out the door, and up the stairs he went. He didn't even give me time to give an answer.

I went into the living room, picked up the papers, ribbons, boxes, and put them into a garbage bag, then carried them outside to the ash pit. In those days, we could burn papers and trash. I lit the papers with a match and went back in the house.

I cleaned the kitchen, washed the dishes, swept the floor, sat down to have a cup of coffee and a cigarette. I looked at the clock - it was seven - he had been gone for three hours. What in the world could he be doing upstairs for three hours? I could only imagine.

I am hurt that he is upstairs and not with me. I am angry and upset. I decided that it was time for him to come back downstairs. I opened the door to the hallway, walked two steps to the stairs, and yelled, "Are you going to come downstairs tonight?"

He opened the door upstairs and yelled, "Yes, in ten minutes!"

Twenty minutes later I yelled at him again, "Your ten minutes are up! When are you coming downstairs?"

"Right now!" he yelled at me.

He came down those stairs two-at-a-time; I could tell he was furious! His face was red, his eyes were glazed with anger, and darker brown than usual. His breath reeked with the smell of beer. He grabbed my shoulder with one hand and slapped my face. The pain was sharp and I could feel the ringing in my ears. He looked at me with an icy stare and cold eyes. "Don't you ever yell at me again, do you understand?" he screamed. "I will be back when I am damn good and ready!"

He turned and went back upstairs. The tears rolled down my checks. I could feel the heat on my face where he had slapped me. I slowly went back inside the apartment, got ready for bed, and cried myself to sleep. I have no idea what time he came back, but he was there in the morning. Deep inside of me I knew I had made the biggest mistake of my life. It was the beginning of the web of deception.

He apologized, he was sorry for what he had done; he didn't know what had come over him. He had to get ready to go back to camp, as he was being transferred from Vail, Colorado, to Fort Carson in Colorado Springs. We would not be together again for six weeks. He was going to take that time to find us an apartment in Colorado Springs. He took me in his arms and tenderly kissed me. "I'm so sorry," he whispered, "I don't know why I did that, and I promise I will never do that again."

I believed him. I loved him. What did I know? I

was sixteen, I believed we knew everything, I had all the answers. I thought I was ten-feet-tall, I was indestructible. I had decided I had enough love for both of us, and I was the right person to teach him what love was.

    I packed our wedding gifts, my clothes, and the few pots and pans that I owned. I wanted to be ready to go to our new apartment. Bob was coming to get me; it was Thursday, and Bob would be here Friday night. I was anxious to start my new life with my husband.

4

We were going to be happy, live in a white cottage with a white picket-fence, a boy for you and a girl for me. The white cottage turned out to be a one-bedroom basement apartment, with no white picket-fence. We had an electric stove, refrigerator, and no kitchen sink. I washed our dishes in the cement tubs where the washer and dryer were located. The rent was fifty-dollars-a-month, and we paid our own electricity. When the first electric bill arrived, I asked Bob, "What is this?"

"It's the electric bill," he replied.

"Oh,'" I said, " and what do you do with it?"

"You pay it."

"Oh, where do you go to pay it?"

His voice was stern as he glared at me. "Don't you know anything? Haven't you ever seen an electric bill? Where have you been, under a rock?"

I placed my hands on my hips and glared at him. "Now, you wait just a minute! I have lived in an apartment all my life. I don't have a clue about electric bills. I have never seen one until now. So now, what does that make me, stupid?"

I could feel the tension mounting as he took a step towards me. He gave me a cold stare. "I have told you before, not to raise your voice. There are serious consequences when you do."

I swallowed hard. I could feel the lump in my throat. "All right," I said. "I'm sorry I got a little snippy about it. Where do I go to pay this bill?"

He gave me the bill. "Take it to Gordon's Pharmacy. It is three blocks from here on Tejon Street. Here is twenty-five dollars for the bill. While you are there, you can apply for a job. I saw a sign in the window a few days ago that read, 'Help Wanted, Counter Girl'. The store opens at eight. It would be a good idea for you to be there."

I could feel the tension in my stomach, and my

throat tightened up. I didn't want my voice to be shaky. I took a deep breath, cleared my throat, said to myself, "Go ahead and ask. He can't do any more than get mad, and raise his voice." "How do I apply for the job? I don't know what to say."

"What is the matter with you?" he demanded. "Don't you know anything? Just go in the store and apply for the job. Is that so hard for you to figure out?" His voice was stern and loud.

I stepped away from him, walked across the room to the bathroom, closed the door, and wiped the tears from my eyes. I was not going to let him see me cry. I blew my nose, stepped out of the bathroom, and decided I could go and apply for the job without his help.

I arrived at the drug store at eight. I was nervous, and my legs felt like they were made of cotton balls. I walked to the counter, opened my purse, took out the electric bill, and placed it on the counter.

"May I help you?" the short gentleman behind the counter asked.

"Yes, you can," I replied. "I would like to pay this bill, and I would like to see Mr. Gordon."

"I am Mr. Gordon. How can I help you?"

I cleared my throat and took a deep breath. "I saw the sign in the window, and I would like to apply for the job."

He looked at me with gentle, blue eyes, a smile on his lips. "Have you any experience?"

"No, I have never had a job."

He looked me over with a curious look. "I see you are married. How old are you?"

I stood up as straight as I could, looked him in the eye, and said, "I am seventeen-years old. "I learn really quick, I'm friendly, and people like me. I have a good personality."

He placed his hand on his chin, and stood there for a few seconds that seemed like a minute. "Well, I think I will take a chance with you. It is easier to train someone who has no experience. Be here in the morning at eight.

Wear a pair of pants and a shirt, nothing fancy. I will show you how things are done. Right now, I want you to fill out the application. Do you have a Social Security card?"

I opened my purse, took out my wallet, showed him my card, filled out the application, and handed it to him. He looked it over. "You have nice handwriting; you did a good job. I will see you in the morning."

"Thank you! Thank you for the job! You won't be disappointed, I promise!"

I was so happy as I skipped home. I just knew Bob was going to be as glad as I was. Five o'clock and Bob came through the door. I could hardly wait to tell him the news that I got a job. "I am so glad you're home. I got the job, and I start at eight in the morning!"

"Okay, how much do you get paid per hour? You start at eight, so what time do you get off work? Do you work on Saturday and Sunday?"

My voice was shaky as I replied, "I didn't ask him. I was so excited about getting the job, I didn't think about all that stuff."

"What is the matter with you? Are you stupid or something? Don't you know anything? You are supposed to ask how much pay per hour, what are the hours, do you work Monday thru Friday? Do you work on the weekends?"

My eyes fill with tears, and there is a lump in my throat - I can barely talk. "How am I supposed to know all that stuff? I have never had a job before. I don't know what to ask and what not to ask."

He glared at me. "That's because you are stupid."

I stepped over to the closet, took my jacket from the hanger, put it on and walked to the front door.

He yelled, "Where do you think you are going?"

"For a walk!" I screamed back at him. "Maybe I will be smarter when I return!"

I walked to the park that was about four blocks away, and sat down on the bench. I took a deep breath.

I wonder what in the world is the matter with him? Nothing I do seems to please him. Everything I do is wrong, and he finds fault with it. I am not sure how long I am going to put up with this stuff. I am going to see how this job works out. Maybe I can save some money, and then I can be on my own. Must be time to go back to the apartment and see if he is still griping and moaning about how stupid he thinks I am.

When I got back, he was gone. That's nice - no note or anything. I don't have a clue where he went. He will come back at some point in time. Time to get ready for bed. Tomorrow is a big day and I start my first job. I set my alarm for six-thirty. I have to be at work at eight and I do not want to be late.

I was awake at six. I don't know what time he came in - I knew he had been drinking as I could smell the stale beer on his breath. I shut the alarm off, went into the bathroom and took a shower, got dressed, fixed my breakfast, ate, and went to work.

"Good morning, Mr. Gordon."

"Good morning, Sandra. I see you are right on time. Come on and I will show you what I want you to do." He showed me how to make coffee, sandwiches, milkshakes, malts, sodas, sundaes, and cokes of all flavors.

My salary was one-dollar-an-hour, fifteen-minute break in the morning, one hour for lunch, fifteen-minute break in the afternoon. I got paid once-a-week on Friday, the lunch counter was closed on Saturday and Sunday. I worked from eight in the morning, until four in the afternoon. It was an easy job, and I was happy.

Things at home were not good. It seemed if I was happy, he was miserable. Nothing was right. He wasn't making enough money in the Army. Of course, he was only a Private First Class and he did not like his Sergeant.

I began to get in touch with my inner feelings: my marriage may not work. I also wanted to do everything I knew to do to make it work. I loved him, and I had no idea that I really had a fierce attachment to him. At some level, which I did not know at the time, he was my ticket to freedom.

I had been working for Mr. Gordon for five months, I was married for the same length of time. I am going to look for a room to rent near where I work. I will spend Thanksgiving holiday in Denver. When I return to Colorado Springs, I will have a place to stay so that I won't be with Bob.

Friday before Thanksgiving, Mr. Gordon told me the lunch counter would be closed the following week. He would pay me on Friday, and give me a week's extra pay to cover Thanksgiving. He had no idea what a favor he was doing for me. Mr. Gordon handed me my paycheck on Friday afternoon. He smiled. "Have a good Thanksgiving, and I will see you next Monday. Are you doing anything special?"

He caught me by surprise. My eyes filled with tears. "I am leaving tonight for Denver. I am not taking my husband with me. He doesn't know I am going. He is so awful to live with. Nothing I do is right. He is not happy about anything."

"Oh, I am sorry to hear that. You looked like you were so happy. I hope you are coming back to work. You are good to have around, and the customers like you."

"Oh yes, I am coming back. I did not mean to burden you with my troubles."

He stepped over to me and placed his arm around my shoulder. "If there is anything I can do for you, please do not hesitate to ask."

As I brushed away the tears, I managed to say, "Thank you."

On my way home, I went to the Greyhound Bus Station and bought a round-trip-ticket to Denver. The bus would be leaving at eight that evening. As I walked home feeling sad and lonely, I kicked a rock down the sidewalk.

I wondered if I could kick Bob in the butt as hard as I could kick that rock. Probably not - he would grab my leg and I would be on the floor. He is supposed to be late tonight; he said he had guard duty. Hope he was telling the truth.

I will have time to get my suitcase packed, and walk to the bus station. If I have a little time, I can get a bite to eat while I am there.

I wonder what he will think when he comes home and

finds I am gone. No note, no nothing. He will probably be angry. So what? He will get over it, or he will be mad for a long time. Am I scared? Yep, I have been scared before, and I will probably be scared again.

I arrived in Denver at ten that evening. Went to the baggage department, picked up my suitcase, caught the bus, and went to where my mother and stepdad were living. By this time, she had married again. His name was Harry. They had bought a house in Southwest Denver.

It was eleven by the time I was ringing the doorbell. Of course, all the lights were out and they were in bed. I rang the bell several times - finally Harry came to the door. He slowly opened the door to see who it was this time of night.

"What are you doing here? It's eleven at night. Where's Bob? What happened?"

"If you will let me in, I'll answer all of your questions."

"Okay, Sander." Harry has always called me Sander. Why? I do not know.

Mother came out into the living room. "What happened? What are you doing here? "

"Stop!" I shouted. "I needed a break from him for a while, so I left."

"What's going to happen now?" my mother yelled.

"I don't know what's going to happen. Furthermore, I don't care. I just know that everything I do is wrong. There is nothing I do that he is happy with."

Mother folded her arms across her chest and cleared her throat. "You know you cannot stay here for more than a few days. I don't want Bob coming up here yelling at me. I can't stand it! I can't fix it! I don't know what to do!"

I knew she would act like this. I thought that maybe, just this one time, she would be different. What in the world was I thinking? I took a step back, looked at my mother. "You do not have to do anything, just go to bed. I will take care of the problem one way or the other. I just need a place to be for a few days."

She turned and glared at me with a wild stare, and went to bed.

I shrugged my shoulders and turned toward Harry. "You might just as well go to bed. I will make myself a bed on the couch. We will talk about all of this stuff in the morning."

"Okay, Sander, I'll see you in the morning."

There is no way I could tell them that our love life is deteriorating. They simply would not understand it. Besides, I wouldn't tell them in the first place. My mother has never helped me with any kind of problem. What makes me think she would help me now? In the morning, I am going to call my friend, Cindy. I am going to see if I stay with her for a few days. I better get to sleep, as morning will come sooner than I want it to.

"Good morning, Sander. Did you sleep well?"

"No," I replied. "I had too much on my mind to sleep well. I feel like a loaded dump-truck. "

Harry looked at me with a blank stare, and I knew he had no idea what I was talking about.

"This is how it is, Harry. I have too much stuff to sort through all at one time. I am going to call Cindy and stay with her for a few days. Maybe Cindy and I can sort this out together."

Oh, my goodness! I completely forgot to look for a room to rent before I left for Denver. I will just have to look for a room when I get back to Colorado Springs.

"Sander, Sander, are you okay?" Harry yelled at me.

"Oh, yes, Harry. I was just thinking about something else. Let's have some breakfast.
Do you have any cold cereal around here?"

"Yes, it's here in the cupboard. Okay, Sander, you can get the milk and I'll get the cereal. I'll even make the coffee."

"Sounds like a good deal to me, Harry."

"After breakfast, I'm going to give Cindy a call, and then I am going to take the bus to her place.

"Hi, Cindy. Are you going to be busy today? I am in town for a few days and I need a place to stay. Can I come over?"

"Sure. What happened? I thought you had moved to Colorado Springs with Bob."

"I did. I'll tell you all about it when I see you this afternoon."

I was getting ready to go when mother came into the room. "Where are going now? You just got here last night, and you're running off already."

"I'm going over to Cindy's for a few days. I'll be back to see you before I go back to Colorado Springs. "

Mother took a deep breath. "By the way, when you showed up here last night, I thought you had left Bob for good. Now you are saying that you are going back to Colorado Springs."

I turned and stared at my mother, wondering where in the world she gets her ideas?
"Mother, I have a job I have to return to. All my belongings are at the apartment. If I decide to leave Bob, I'll rent a room close to where I work."

Her eyes became huge. She stared at me with that familiar wild stare, and began to wring her hands and pace the floor. "What am I going to do? He will blame me, I just know it. It'll be my fault. I told you to leave him."

I shouted at her, "Mother, stop it! This is nonsense! I haven't left him yet. I said IF I decide to leave him. Will you listen for just a minute? Today is Saturday, and I don't have to be back to work until next Monday. For all I know, Bob may show up here for Thanksgiving. I simply don't know what will happen. Just calm down! I need to leave - the bus will be here shortly. I'll call you when I get to Cindy's."

I ran to catch the bus. *Oh, great. There is no place to sit. I get to stand up and balance this suitcase. Looks like this is going to be a neat little trick.* A young man got up and offered me his seat. I thanked him and sat down.

I wonder why there are so many people on the bus on Saturday? Maybe they are going downtown to shop for Thanksgiving. I am sure glad I do not have to transfer to another bus. When I get off the bus, I will have to walk two blocks. This suitcase gets heavy after a while.

Here is my stop. I rang the bell, and got off the bus when it came to a stop. I am sure glad that it is not raining or snowing today. The sun was shining. I kicked a leaf or two as I walked along. I walked up the four steps to Cindy's, rang the doorbell, and waited for her to answer. Seems like it's taking her a long time to get to the door. Oh, I see her coming, as I peek through the curtain.

"Oh, Sandra, I am so glad to see you!" Cindy screeched as she put her arms around me. "How are you? What has happened that you've left Bob? I thought everything was going to be so perfect for the two of you."

"Slow down, Cindy, and let me catch my breath. First of all, you asked me how I am. To answer that question, I feel like a loaded dump-truck with no place to go to get rid of my load. Second question, what happened that you don't know? I just know that everything I do is wrong. He's not happy about anything. Third question, everything was going to be so perfect. Good luck with that kind of thinking. Is your mother home?"

Cindy looked at me with one raised eyebrow. "Of course, she's home - it's only one in the afternoon. She's concerned about you, Sandra. Come on, let's go upstairs. My mother wants to talk to you."

5

Rose, Cindy's mother, was born in Russia. She is Jewish, born with a broken left arm, which is crooked. It looked like it had a stroke - it was limp, her wrist was bent, and her fingers are always closed.

"Come in, Sandra, I am so glad to see you," Rose said with a smile. "Tell me what happened."

"First of all, I don't know what happened. I just know things are not going like I had planned. I want my freedom. I want to be on my own. I want to do what I want to do. He wants to order me around. He thinks he is the boss. I can't do anything right; I don't know how to cook; I don't clean the house right; the laundry isn't done right. Nothing is right."

Rose placed her hand on her hip, and gave me one of her stern looks. "This is the way it is. Both of you girls had no business getting married at the age of sixteen and seventeen. Neither one of you know what life is really all about. So, what makes you think you are going to live happily ever after? Marriage is not based on love and mush, for heaven sakes. It's a lot of work, and you have to work together."

"Then why did you let Cindy get married at seventeen if she was too young? Will you tell me that?"

"Sandra, for your information, Cindy would not get off my back until I gave my consent for her to get married. If your marriage and Cindy's don't work, both of you will have to pay the consequences."

"Oh, great, now we have consequences to pay. Let me tell you this: for your information, I have enough love for Bob and me. All he needs is a good woman to show him what love is all about."

Rose turned and gave me a puzzled look. "There is no point in talking to you about the situation, because you already have it all figured out. If you will excuse me, I'll be in the kitchen making some sandwiches for lunch."

There is no way I am going to confide in Cindy's mother. She would just ridicule me and tell me again that I was too young to get married in the first place. I think I will ask Cindy if she wants to go out for coffee after a while. I can't talk to her while her mother is around. Rose thinks I don't know anything, anyway.

"Okay, girls, lunch is ready. Come in the kitchen."

"Oh good, you made my favorite - ham and cheese, good coffee, and chocolate cake."

"Cindy, we've had our lunch. Let's go for a walk."

"I'll go and get my jacket and be right back."

Rose yelled at Cindy, "Just where do you think you are going?"

"I'm going for a walk with Sandra!" Cindy screamed at her mother.

Cindy slammed the door as we left. I could tell she was ticked-off at her mother. "Why does she have to know every move I make? For crying out loud, I am a married woman, and she is still asking me where are you going, what are you doing, and why are you doing it?"

I shrugged my shoulders. "I don't know, Cindy, maybe your mother is just nosy."

Cindy raised one eyebrow. "She IS nosy, and I would like it if she would learn to mind her own business."

I stopped walking, and looked at Cindy with one of my stern looks. "I don't think that is going to happen in this lifetime. She has been minding your business since the day you were born. She will continue to mind your business as long as you live with her."

Cindy raised her voice to a high pitch. "Are you telling me I'm going to have to move, in order to get my mother off my back?"

I looked her square in the eye. "Pretty much, Cindy. You can't expect to live here with your mother and expect her to mind her own business, when she pays for everything and you get a free ride."

Cindy screamed at me, "I don't know if I can live on my own! I'm scared! I've always been with my mother!"

I yelled at her: "For crying out loud! Here you are, living with your mother, eighteen-years-old, married, and she pays for everything, including your cigarettes. I get the idea you think it's okay because you are scared. You are a wimp. Let's quit this conversation. We're not going to get anywhere. If we continue this way we will end up mad at each other. Let's talk about something else."

Cindy agreed. "How about if you tell me what you are going to do about Bob?"

I cleared my throat. I was not sure how I was going to answer that question. I was awake for a long time last night mulling over in my mind what I was going to do.

"Cindy, I'm not sure yet. I know I have to go back to Colorado Springs after Thanksgiving, to my job. Depending on how things are with Bob, I'm thinking about looking for a room close to where I work. I love him dearly, but I can't figure out what in the world I have done to make him act the way he does."

Cindy put her arm around my shoulder. "What makes you think it's something you have done to make him act the way he does? Come on, Sandra, let's go back to the house. Maybe he's called looking for you."

My eyes filled with tears. Well, maybe he'll call, he could be worried; however, I doubt it. He will probably be ticked-off because I left and didn't leave a note."

6

Bob showed up at Cindy's house. Of course, the first words out of his mouth were, "How come you didn't leave me a note?"

"Is there a reason why I have to leave you a note? You don't seem to think it's important for you to tell me where you've gone."

"Yes, you should have told me that you left town. I didn't leave town. I only went to the base."

"Well, good for you. Now, how is that different? It is only different when I don't tell you."

His face took on a gentle look, his tone of voice was softer. "What happened that you decided to leave?"

I cleared my throat; all of a sudden, I was nervous and scared. I clasped my hands together. "It's like this: nothing I do is right. You seem to find fault with everything."

I had made myself a promise - I wasn't going to cry or get emotional. All of a sudden, my throat tightened, my heart was pounding, and there was not enough air to breathe. The tears rolled down my cheeks.

He stepped over to me, wrapped his arms around me, held me gently in his arms, and I cried. I knew my heart was breaking. He gently lifted my chin, looked into my eyes. "I don't know what came over me. I am so sorry. I don't mean to do what I do. Please come back to me. I'll be better."

I melted like a snowball on a warm winter day. I knew I loved him dearly. I had no idea what a dear price I would pay.

It seemed easy for him to be charming. He could slip in and out of his charm as easily as putting on a jacket. Bob had a puzzled look on his face when he asked about Thanksgiving. "Where are we going to spend the holiday? Do you have any ideas, Sandra?"

Cindy looked at me, then looked at Bob. "Well," she said, "Mother has a turkey, and I know she plans on cooking it. Why don't you two guys just plan on staying here for dinner tomorrow?"

Bob smiled. "That sounds like a good idea to me." He glanced at me. "What do you think about that, Sandra?"

"Sounds good to me. I will help Rose with the cooking."

We had a good dinner on Thanksgiving, played some games, told jokes, laughed and enjoyed each other. I called my mother and wished her a good day. I told her that Bob was here and I would be going back to Colorado Springs with him. We will be over on Sunday for a visit in the morning. We will be leaving in the afternoon for home. She did not make any comment, didn't ask any questions, and I did not give out any information.

He was in the honeymoon stage; everything went well until after Christmas, when things began to fall apart. I couldn't do anything right. I could not cook, clean, do the laundry, iron his clothes, or even wash the dishes. I'm sure I didn't know how to flush the toilet and do it right!

I began to wonder about my sanity. Many afternoons, as I would walk home from work, I would ask myself, "How long was I willing to put up with all this stuff? What in the world am I doing wrong? No matter how many times I tried to put the pieces together, they didn't fit. There was either too many pieces or not enough. I was never able to figure out which way it was supposed to go."

It was January when I decided I would leave Bob in June. Only this time, I'd move back to Denver, get a job, and a place of my own. I started to save a little money for my new life without him. He must have sensed I was planning something, as he started to improve. All of a sudden, he was sweet and kind. I began to wonder why I was thinking about leaving him. It was May, and I was on cloud nine. Bob was wonderful, cooperative, and he couldn't do enough for me. We were planning to go to Portland for the month of August.

August 1st, 1957, we left Colorado Springs for our vacation. It was a warm summer day, light breeze, blue sky, just right for traveling. When we entered the Columbia River Gorge, and I saw the Columbia River for the first time, I was overwhelmed with its beauty, the force of the river - it was majestic. When we got past Hood River, and I saw all the green trees, lush grass, the beauty of the parks, and the waterfalls, I was mesmerized.

On August 3rd, we arrived in Portland. It was a warm, sunny afternoon. Maynard and Susie lived at 6414 S.E. 72nd St. When I saw the house, and went inside with Bob, I thought they were rich. Never had I known anyone who had a freezer full of food. There was meat, frozen corn, strawberries, blackberries, and swiss chard that I thought was spinach. *"Wow! What a deal!" I thought to myself: "I've hit the jackpot! I will never be without something to eat again!"*

We had dinner that evening which consisted of hamburgers and French fries. Everyone else had beer to drink, but I was too young, so I drank a bottle of pop.

The following day, we went to the coast. I was hypnotized. The flowing of the river, the trees, the lush green valley, scenery I had never seen before. When we arrived at Seaside, and I stood for the first time and gazed at the ocean, it was a scene I could hardly believe. Here I stood, looking at the ocean on a piece of land, and the rest of what I saw was water.

Bob was loving, kind, gentle, and charming. I couldn't imagine why I was planning to leave him. He acted like he couldn't get enough of me. We left Portland on the 17th of August, to return to Colorado Springs. I went back to work, and Bob went back to his duties at the Army Base. Things went along very smoothly for several weeks.

It was the middle of September when I discovered I was pregnant. Oh, boy, here I was, eighteen-years-old, and I was going to have a baby. Things were beginning to fall apart again and I was planning to leave.

I was in a panic, scared, and didn't know what to do. Bob was griping again - I couldn't do anything right. "How come you are sick to your stomach every day? Why don't you go to the doctor and find out what is wrong with you?" I didn't want to tell him that I was going to have a baby! Of course, I don't know for sure, because

I haven't been to the doctor yet. So why don't I quit worrying and thinking about it, make an appointment and find out for sure? I'm scared! I don't know how he is going to feel about becoming a father!

The first part of October, I went to the doctor; it was confirmed I was going to have a baby the first part of May. I had it all figured out in my mind - Bob was going to be so happy that he was going to be a daddy. Wrong. He was okay, he just wasn't overjoyed about the coming event.

Bob was due to get discharged from the Army in June. We decided I would take the train from Colorado Springs to Portland in April. We thought it would be better for me to have the baby in Portland. On a Sunday morning in April, I boarded the train for Portland. Tuesday afternoon, I was met at the train station. I was excited - I had a mother-in-law and a father-in-law, and they were going to take good care of me until Bob would be home.

I was in for a big surprise. My mother-in-law, Susie, had a drinking problem. Her husband, Maynard, worked in the construction business as a truck-driver.

A few days after my arrival, it was early in the morning. I was having my second cup of coffee and my third cigarette. Maynard hadn't left for work, as he was waiting for his brother, Wayne, to come by and pick him up. They rode together when they were working on the same job, as they worked for the same company. Wayne was a shovel operator.

Maynard had just told me his brother was coming to give him a ride. "I want you to meet him when he comes." Just as those words came out of his mouth, Wayne rapped on the door. "Come in, Wayne. I want you to meet my daughter-in law."

Wayne stepped forward. He was almost six-feet-tall, dark-brown hair, and warm brown eyes. He had a firm handshake, broad shoulders, a gentle voice, and a warm smile. I noticed his eyes twinkled when he smiled. He shook my hand. "When is the baby due?" he asked.

I smiled at him and said, "In about two weeks. To be precise, the 5th of May. Every morning, when Wayne would come by to pick up Maynard, he would always ask, "How are you today?" His gentleness made an impression on me.

Susie was making her daily trips to the local tavern. Every night, the fight between Maynard and Susie would be on.

Tuesday, May 6th, at six a.m., I was having labor pains. Susie and Maynard were up and ready to take me to the hospital. Maynard dropped Susie and me at the hospital and went to work. I was put in a room, checked by the nurse, and then it was time for me to go to work on having a baby. At four that afternoon, I had a baby girl. I was alone, scared, eighteen, husband still in the Army. He would not arrive until Sunday. Susie had left hours ago. She had made several phone calls and found a friend to take her to the tavern.

Sunday, May 11th, was Mother's Day, 1958. It's time for the baby and me to go home. When Susie and Maynard arrived at the hospital, they brought a surprise with them. They brought Bob. I was so happy and delighted to see him. He seemed pleased to see his new baby girl, Cheryl, for the first time. He wrapped his arms around me, and kissed me in the old familiar way.

We arrived at the house and unpacked the items from the car. I placed Cheryl in her new crib. Bob stood and gazed at his new baby girl. I could tell for the moment he was pleased.

Susie informed everyone it was time for a celebration. "So, let's go to the tavern!" Of course, I couldn't go - I was only eighteen. Charming Bob stepped over to me, took me in his arms, "Oh, you don't mind do you, if we go out and have a few beers?"

"Oh, of course not," I replied. I knew it wouldn't do any good to say anything else. I also knew it would be more than a few beers. They would either come home happy with each other, or in a big fight. They left, and I made myself a sandwich, drank coffee, watched T.V., and took care of the baby. I was probably asleep when they came home.

    We lasted two months. Bob and his mother were out drinking one night, when they got into a yelling match and Bob slapped her face. They were still fighting when they came home. Susie informed Bob he had one week to move. "Take your wife and baby with you, or I will have the sheriff come and escort you to a new location!"

7

The following morning, we went looking for an apartment. We found one on S.E 35th and Alder Ct. It was furnished, and we moved that afternoon. Bob's family system was not a good one. Of course, I didn't take that into consideration when I married him. Those kinds of things were not part of my thinking process. Susie's husband, Maynard, was her fifth husband.

This is the story that Bob told me: His mother was married to Jim, and had two boys together, Bob and his brother Jim. His dad, Jim, was in the hospital with a broken back. Susie wanted to join the Army. She was a nurse. While he was in the hospital, she joined the Army. She said she was single and had no children. Bob was three, and his brother Jim, was two. She left them alone in the house. The boys were hungry so Bob stole some milk from the neighbor. When it was discovered they were alone, the police were called. The boys were taken into custody, and placed in foster care. From that time on, the boys were in-and-out of foster care. Susie and Jim got a divorce. He married four more times. By the time I came into the family scene, he was married for the fifth time.

It was now time for me to meet Bob's dad, Jim. Jim had not seen Bob for a long time. Bob's brother, Jim, had divorced the family system and moved back east. I met Jim once-or-twice before I married Bob. His brother told me I was going to be sorry that I married him. He drinks, and he will never go to church with you. Did I believe him? Of course not.

Bob was anxious for me to meet his dad; he wanted him to see his new baby. I wondered what this was going to be like. His mother told us to move. It was going to be interesting to see what his dad was like. I found out his dad was hot-tempered, and still had an ax to grind with Susie.

The first words out of his mouth were, that if he wanted a woman who drank at the bar, he would've bought a bar. It was okay if they drank at home, but not okay if they drank in public. I wondered at the time, "What's the difference? If you like to drink, what did it matter if you drank at home, or in public?"

I was introduced to Jim and Naomi, Jim's fifth wife. Jim was a stocky-built man, about five-feet-ten-inches tall. Black hair, brown eyes, gruff voice, hard-working man, with calluses on his hands. He had a critical eye as he shook my hand and looked me over. Naomi had fire-engine red hair, brown eyes, fair skin, and let me know she had a temper to match her hair. She went on to tell me that she drank at home. I thought at the time, that was rather odd. I didn't care if she drank at home, or in public. We didn't stay very long; they looked the baby over as if she was under inspection.

Bob found employment, working at an electric motor shop. Things were going smoothly between us. We moved from the apartment on S.E. Alder, to a house on N. Campbell St. It was a house that Bob rented from his uncle. It contained two bedrooms, a small living room, a good-sized kitchen, and was heated with oil.

It was a warm September evening, and we had just finished dinner. Cheryl was four-months-old. Bob looked across the table at me; Cheryl was on my lap. "I just found out today where my ex-stepmother, Eileen, lives with her husband, Matson. You'll like her. She's a lot of fun. I have to tell you, I'm anxious to see her. I haven't seen her since I was about fourteen.

He went on to say: "Now that I'm twenty-three, I look a little bit different than I did when I was a teenager. As I was leaving work today, my stepsister, Sharon, came into the workshop. Eileen is her mother, and Jim is her dad. She gave me their address, and said she knew her mother would be glad to see me. I told her I was married and had a baby girl."

I was puzzled. "How long has it been since you've seen your stepsister?"

He put his hand to his lips. "Let me see. Probably about nine years."

I stood up with Cheryl, and looked at Bob. "Was

she glad to see you?"

"Well, not really," he said with a frown. "That's another story I'll tell you another day. Let's get the baby ready to go and we will go over tonight. It's not very far from here. They live in the housing project, Columbia Villa."

"What is this place?" I asked Bob. He glanced at me with a frown. "This is the housing project."

As I was looking the place over, I observed the green grass that was neatly cut and trimmed. Nice small hedges, beautiful flowers: red, orange, yellow, violet - what a lovely place! I glanced at Bob. "This would be a nice place to live."

He grinned. "Maybe we will move here sometime."

I thought to myself, *"This is going to be interesting; I wonder if Eileen is anything like Naomi or Susie? I wonder what her husband is like."* I didn't have time to ask Bob, as we were just pulling into their driveway.

I was a little nervous as I looked at Bob. "Do you think Eileen will be glad to see you?"

He cleared his throat. "I don't know. We're going to find out in about two minutes."

Bob knocked on the door. A man of about five-feet-six, with reddish-brown hair, opened the door. "What can I do for you?" he asked in a gruff voice. Bob stepped back. "I am looking for a lady by the name of Eileen. My name is Bob."

Eileen rolled up in her wheelchair beside the man. "Oh, my goodness, Bob, come in. Matson, this is my stepson, Bob." Bob bent down to hug her and she put her arms around him. "I'm so glad to see you. Who's this you have with you?"

Bob gave me a quick look. "This is my wife Sandra, and our baby, Cheryl."

"I must have known we were going to have company tonight. I just made a pot of coffee, and took some brownies out of the oven," Eileen said with a smile on her face. "By the way Matson, do we have any vanilla ice-cream?" Matson stepped over to the freezer, opened the door, looked inside, and took out the ice-cream.

We had chocolate brownies, vanilla ice-cream, good coffee, good conversation and a great time. I liked them both. They were homey and down-to-earth. They took turns holding the baby. Cheryl got fussy and wanted her bottle. Eileen wanted to feed her. I placed the baby in her arms, and gave the warm bottle to Eileen.

Eileen looked her over. "What a beautiful baby! Bob, can I be her grandma?"

Bob stepped over to Eileen, and placed his hand on her shoulder. "Of course, you can. I am sure you'll be a better grandma than my mother Susie, or my stepmother, Naomi."

Eileen looked at him with a frown. "I was your stepmother once."

"Wait a minute, Eileen. "You've always been a good mother to me. My own mother left me and my brother, Jimmy, when we were very young. She didn't return until I was fifteen-years-old. By the way, Eileen, what happened to you that has put you in a wheelchair?"

Her eyes filled with tears, her voice shaky, and she cleared her throat. "After your dad and I were divorced, I was diagnosed with multiple sclerosis. My legs wouldn't hold me up. The muscles in my legs became too weak. I've been in this chair for five years. When I want to stand for a little bit, I have some braces I put on my legs."

"Do the braces help?" Bob wanted to know.

Eileen glanced at Matson. "Let's give Bob and Sandra a demonstration as to how these braces work."

"Okay," he said. "I'll get the braces, and you can wheel yourself into the bedroom. I'll help you get on the bed. By the way, you should've had these on a long time ago. You are supposed to wear these for six hours every day."

"Yes, I know, Mr. Matson. You, my friend, don't have a clue how warm I can get with these braces on."

Eileen wheeled herself to the side of the bed. Matson stepped into the living-room. "Come on into the bedroom. I'll show you how I get Eileen onto the bed."

Bob looked things over. "You are pretty good with that wheelchair, Eileen."

She looked at him with a smile. "I should be - I've had five years of practice. Okay, Matson, let's get this show on the road." He stepped in front of her, bent his knees, and wrapped his arms around her waist. She wrapped her arms around his waist, and on the count of three, they stood together. They took two steps to the left and he placed her on the side of the bed. There were two straps on each brace, one above the knee, one below. She slipped her foot into the shoe that was attached to the brace, buckled the straps, and put the other brace on. In a sitting position, the braces would be bent at the knee; when Eileen stood up, the braces automatically locked into place.

"Okay, Matson, put me in the wheelchair."

Bob stepped over to Eileen. "It's time for us to go home. Six a.m. comes quickly. I have to be to work at eight"

Eileen grabbed his arm. "Wait just a minute. I want to know when you kids are coming back? What are you doing on Saturday?"

Bob gave me a quick glance. "What are we doing on Saturday, Sandra?"

I smiled at him. "Nothing that I know about - we can come over anytime."

Bob placed his hand on Eileen's. "We'll see you on Saturday."

8

It was a cold November morning. Cheryl had just turned six-months-old. We were out of oil to heat the house. Bob had gone to work. I was furious with him, as he knew we would be out of oil by morning. I had told him about it the day before. He wasn't concerned. I had no money, didn't know how to drive, and had no car. Bob had two cars.

I knew I couldn't stay all day in a cold house with a baby. I dressed myself and Cheryl, packed the diaper-bag with diapers, change of clothes, and bottles of formula. Cheryl and I left for Eileen's and Matson's house. We lived on 59th and N. Campbell, and they lived in Columbia Villa on Woolsey Ave. It was six miles away.

It was cold outside, the wind was blowing, but I was thankful it wasn't raining. I walked and walked. I thought my arms were going to break. Two-and-a-half-hours later, we made it. I rang the doorbell. Matson opened the door. "What in the world are you doing here, at this time of day? Where is Bob? Get in here, you look frozen. Here, give the baby to me and you take your coat off."

I explained to Matson and Eileen, what had happened. Bob knew we were low on oil. "We were here on Monday evening, and this is only Wednesday. I don't know what is wrong with Bob. I can't keep the baby in a cold house all day with no heat. He thought I could stay in the kitchen all day with the oven on. Now, how long is the oven going to heat the house? That doesn't make a bit of sense to me."

Eileen looked at me with a stern glance. "Come into the kitchen. I know you probably haven't had any breakfast."

"I'll be there in just a minute-or-two. I need to put a blanket on the floor for the baby."

Eileen fixed me scrambled eggs with cheddar cheese, toast and coffee. I washed the dishes, while Matson helped Eileen put her braces on. It was time for

Cheryl to take a nap. I rocked her to sleep, while Matson fixed a bed for her on the couch.

Eileen folded her arms in front of her chest, and looked at me with a concerned look in her eyes. "Okay, Sandra, it's time for you to tell me what is really going on with Bob. Remember this: I was his stepmother once, and I know how difficult he can be."

I took a deep breath, leaned back in my chair. I could feel my eyes filling with tears. The last thing I wanted to do was cry.

Matson stepped over to me, and placed his hand in mine. "It's okay if you cry. I'm sure things are not easy for you."

I looked up at him. "I simply don't know what to do. One thing I do know, is that I'm planning to leave him again. He's not happy and neither am I. I don't know how much longer I can put up with him. I don't do anything right. Today is just about the last straw. He wasn't concerned that we would run out of oil. He just figured I could keep the baby warm in the kitchen. Just keep the oven on and everything will be okay."

"What is wrong with him?" Eileen wanted to know.

I glanced at her. "If I had the answer to that question maybe I could fix him. The problem is, I don't have the answer."

Eileen was concerned. "Does Bob know where you and the baby went?"

"Yes," I replied, "I left him a note. Maybe he will feel bad that I had to walk six miles with a baby, to stay warm."

Eileen raised one eyebrow. "Well, when he gets here tonight, I'm going to give him a piece of my mind. He's not going to like what I'm going to say. He has no business leaving my grandbaby in a cold house. His first job is to see that his baby is well taken care of. As far as I'm concerned, he's not doing his job."

"I hope he will listen to you. He doesn't seem to care about how I feel about anything. He only seems to be interested in himself and what he wants. He thinks he needs two cars; in case one of them breaks down, he can use the parts from the other car to repair it. I don't know how much sense that makes, but it makes no sense to me. You see, I'm just a woman, so what do I know about fixing cars?"

Bob showed up about six. I could tell he was mad, by the way he pulled up to the house, slammed on his brakes, and slammed the car door when he got out. He took long strides to the door, and didn't bother to knock or ring the doorbell. He jerked the door open, and took a long step inside the house. "Just what the hell are you doing over here?"

Eileen rolled into the room in her wheelchair. "Wait just a minute there, Mr. Bob. First of all, you have no business talking to her like that. Number two, this house is nice and warm. Sandra and the baby can come here to a warm place."

His eyes were darker brown. I knew he wasn't happy. "Hell no!" he yelled. I don't have any money for oil. I don't get paid until Friday, and this is only Wednesday! You got any money I can borrow until Friday?"

"Will twenty-bucks help you?" Eileen wanted to know.

Eileen gave Bob twenty-dollars. Bob looked at me. "Are you coming with me?"

"No," I replied. "When you get the house warmed up, you can come back and get the baby and me. I'm not coming home until the house is warm."

He glared at me. "Why, you little bitch!"

Eileen yelled at him: "You are the one who's in the wrong here! You have created the problem. Don't take your stuff out on your wife because you failed your duty as a husband and father. Get your butt out of here, and get the house warmed up! I don't want to hear any more from you!"

"Okay, okay, I'm going." He slammed the door when he left.

He came back in an hour to take the baby and me home. He wasn't happy about the fact I told Eileen and Matson there was no oil to heat the house. He couldn't figure out what the big deal was. After all, we had an oven in the kitchen, and why couldn't I keep the baby warm? Anybody with half-a-brain could've done it. He didn't know what in the world was the matter with me.

A few days later, he came home in a rotten mood. He was complaining that his boss had been on his butt all day. He wasn't rewinding the electric motors at a fast enough pace. He wasn't going to put up with that kind of treatment. He was on a roll by the way he yelled: "What have you been doing all day? There is dust on the windows sills, the windows need to be washed, there is laundry to do, and my dinner isn't ready!"

I placed my hands on my hips. I raised my voice, "That's enough of that yelling of yours. For your information, the baby has had a tummy-ache all day. I have rocked and walked the floor trying to get her settled down. I don't need you to come home in a foul mood. Furthermore, I don't need you to ask me what I've been doing all day. As far as I'm concerned, it's none of your damn business!"

He came over close to me, and raised his hand. "I outta' slap your face so you'll get the message who's in charge here."

I lowered my voice, and looked him square in the eye. "If you do, I'll call the police and I'll press charges against you, and you will go to jail." My insides were shaking as if there was a jack-
hammer inside of my stomach. I was terrified. "By the way, I talked to my mother today. I told her I wanted to come home for Thanksgiving. She said okay."

His voice was softer, "How are you going to get to Denver?"

I glanced at him, cleared my throat. "I can take the bus. I've already checked to see how much the fare is, what time it leaves, and when it will arrive in Denver."

He raised his voice a little. "Just where is the

money coming from?"

"Oh, oh," I thought, "here it comes, for sure. He can't do any more than knock me out for this one." I mustered up my courage, and looked him in the eye. "You have two cars. You can sell one of them."

His face turned red, his eyes got bigger, he raised his voice. "I'm not selling one of my cars so you can go to Denver on the bus for Thanksgiving. Who in the hell do you think you are?"

I shrugged my shoulders. "I can have a talk with Eileen and Matson - maybe they will have a different opinion."

He glared at me. "Okay, I know a guy who wants to buy one of my cars. He works across the street from where I do. I'll talk to him in the morning. When do you want to leave?"

I gave him a smile. "Friday evening at six. Will you take us to the bus station?"

I could tell by the look on his face that he was not happy. He walked over to the couch, sat down with a deep sigh, crossed his legs, folded his arms in front of his chest, and cleared his throat. "I'll take you and the baby to the bus station on Friday. I'm not pleased with this turn of events."

I gave him a stern look. "I wasn't happy when I had to walk six miles with the baby to keep us warm for the day." That was the end of our conversation. Cheryl was already in bed asleep; I went to bed. I couldn't sleep. I tossed and turned, my body was tense, and I was upset. I could feel the tears on my cheeks. I didn't want him to know I was crying.

I was hurt, sad and lonely inside. Deep inside of me, I knew this marriage was not going to work. I know I had to try as hard as I know how, to make this work. If it doesn't, I will know I did everything I could. I wonder why I keep lying to myself?

Morning came sooner than I wanted it to. I didn't sleep well. I still felt nervous and tense.

"Interesting," I decided. *"I have the same old feelings I had when I was a kid at the breakfast table. Always wondering when the bomb was going to drop. Feeling like a violin string that is wound too tight. No point in mulling this over again. I have to get ready to go tomorrow."*

Bob took us to the bus station. He was quiet, seemed to be deep in thought. While we waited for the bus, he slipped his arm around me, pulled me to him and whispered in my ear, "I'm sorry for the way I've been acting. I don't know what happens to me. I love you so much I don't know what I would do without you. You and the baby are my world." He kissed me goodbye. "Please be careful. I'll miss you and the baby."

We waved to each other as the bus pulled away. The tears were flowing down my cheeks. I sat in the seat, held Cheryl in my arms. I began to question myself once again. *"Why was I wondering about my marriage again? He was so wonderful just now. I love him so much, I don't know if I can live without him. I feel confused. Somedays it is very clear in my mind that I want to leave him, and have a life without him. Those are the days when I have it all planned out. When he tells me how much he loves me, I am puzzled one more time. Funny how I let him talk me into buying a one-way ticket. He promised he would come and get us the day after Thanksgiving. He just wants to be with us forever. Such a smooth talker he is. Sounds so wonderful when he says, "But baby doll! I love you so much!"*

I took a deep breath and let it out slowly, my body starting to relax. I laid Cheryl in the seat next to me, closed my eyes, and asked God to protect us as we went on our way. We arrived in Denver, early Sunday morning. It was a good trip. Cheryl slept most of the way - I was glad she was still little. Only six-months-old.

As the bus pulled into the bus station, I could see the taxi cabs were lined up, ready for passengers. I found a cab, got into the back seat with Cheryl, and told the cab driver the address. Thirty minutes later, I was knocking on the door where my mother and Harry lived. My sister, Karen, opened the door. I was so glad to see her. She wrapped her arms around me, shouted for Mother and Harry, to come into the living room.

"Just look at this beautiful baby! Look at her

gorgeous red hair, her soft blue eyes! She is perfect!" Karen had taken Cheryl from my arms, and handed the baby to her grandma. Mother held the baby and gazed into her blue eyes. "My, my, what a nice baby."

I was spellbound with the moment. I felt paralyzed, as if my body parts would not move. I have never known my mother to take an interest in much of anything. My goodness, she likes the baby.

Mother gave me a swift glance. "You know, this is my first grandchild." She stood and rocked Cheryl back-and-forth. She seemed to be in a trance. Harry stepped over to Mother. "Here, let me hold the baby for a while." She turned and gave him the baby.

Karen glanced around the room, turned to go into the kitchen. "You know, I think it's time for some breakfast."

I stepped over to Harry, took Cheryl from his arms. "I'm going to put a blanket on the floor for Cheryl. She can play for a while, while I go and help Karen fix breakfast."

We got through breakfast and washed the dishes. I fed Cheryl her breakfast, that consisting of cereal with applesauce, gave her a bottle, and got her ready for her nap. I put her in the bedroom on the bed, propped pillows around her so she would not roll off the bed. She was tired, and asleep within five minutes.

I stood beside the bed, gazing at this beautiful baby I was responsible for. I am nineteen-years-old. I'm a mother. I was lost in the moment of time.

My childhood friend, Joyce, her mother, Cless, and her dad, Glen, will be glad to see my baby, Cheryl. They have always been good to my sisters and me, when they were our neighbors. I used to say they lived on the right side of the tracks, while we lived on the wrong side. They lived on 17th and Downing St. We lived on 18th and Marion, just a block-and-half away. Their neighborhood was different: houses and trees. Ours was an apartment building, and run-down houses, fences that needed fixing, broken windows, and broken lives. Life was peaceful on

Downing Street. Life on Marion Street was full of chaos.

Karen and I fixed Thanksgiving dinner. It was wonderful. Roasted turkey, baked ham, mashed potatoes, gravy, dressing, green beans, vegetable salad, pickles, olives, carrots, celery sticks, and pumpkin pie. We were stuffed.

9

Friday morning, I called Joyce. "Oh, Sandra!" Joyce screeched into the phone, "Where are you?"

"I'm at my mother's house. I want to know if you are going to be home later today? Karen and I want to come over and show you my baby. Her name is Cheryl."

"You better come over. I'll go tell my mother. She will be so happy to see you and Karen. Come for lunch, my dad will be here. I know they will want to see the baby."

"Okay, Joyce we will see you today about one."

Karen and I took the baby over to see Joyce, Cless, and Glen. We had lunch, good conversation, and a wonderful time. Cless wanted to know when Bob was coming to Denver, and if I was going to go back to Portland. I told her that I was expecting to see Bob on Saturday, and that I would be going back to Portland with him. We would probably leave early Sunday morning. We said our goodbyes, and took the bus to Mother's house.

The following morning, at six a.m., there was a loud knock at the front door. I sat up in bed with a jolt, wondering who in the world was at the door, at this time of day? I peeked through the blind, and there on the porch stood my darling Bob. I rushed to the door, opened it. He pulled me to him, kissed me with a passionate kiss.

He held me in his arms. "I missed you and the baby. I haven't slept good since you left."

I stepped back and looked at him. "I missed you too. The baby and I have slept good together. I've missed your kisses." He came into the house, and we went into the bedroom where Cheryl was sound asleep in my bed.

He stood and gazed at Cheryl, as if seeing her for the first time. He glanced at me with tears in his eyes. "I really didn't know how much I missed you and the baby, until this moment."

I wrapped my arms around him, and kissed him on the cheek. "How about if I go and fix us some breakfast?"

He pulled me to him. "Don't go right now. Lay down with me and the baby. I need a nap. We can have breakfast later." Bob was sound asleep in five minutes. Cheryl began to stir; I picked her up and took her out into the living-room. I cleaned her up, took her into the kitchen, and sat her in the highchair that my stepdad, Harry, had bought for her at Goodwill.

It was three in the afternoon, when Bob finally got up. I had everything packed up and ready to go so we could leave for Portland. I scrambled some eggs, toast, and coffee. I sat down beside him.

"What time do you want to leave in the morning? I called Cindy, and she wanted to know if we could come over for dinner tonight? I told her I would ask you about it, and I would call her later to let her know."

He took a sip of his coffee, looked at me over the rim of his coffee mug. "We can go over to Cindy's house tonight. I want to come back here about ten. We need to leave about six in the morning. We can eat breakfast later."

I pushed my chair back. "Okay, then I'll give Cindy a call, and let her know we'll see her later."

Cindy and her mother, Rose, were delighted with the baby. They took turns playing with Cheryl. We had burgers and salad for dinner. It was soon time for us to go, so that we could get ready to leave in the morning. Cindy, Rose and I said our goodbyes, and wiped our tears.

We had a good night sleep, packed the car, and were ready to leave at six. Mother and Harry were at the front door, ready to tell us their goodbyes. Mother hugged and kissed the baby, gave me a quick hug, turned and went into the kitchen. Harry slipped his arm around my shoulder. I kissed him on the cheek. Harry smiled when he said, "Sander, you guys come back again."

As I sat in the car, closed in with my thoughts and feelings, there seemed to be no escape from the feeling of loneliness. *There was always something I was missing that I couldn't put my finger on. Maybe it was my mother's emotions. Her body was present, but her mind seemed to be lost. Was I missing something? Maybe I will never know. It seems to be something that hangs on my shoulders, just out of reach, with no words to describe it.*

We stopped in Cheyenne, Wyoming, for breakfast. Cheryl slept most of the way, after she had her cereal and her milk. We drove as far as the Idaho border before stopping for the night. We arrived home at two a.m. Tuesday morning. Wednesday, Bob went back to work; it was back to the routine once again.

Bob seemed to be happy - I was wondering how long it was going to last. I didn't have to wait very long. Saturday morning, the car was sounding funny, according to Bob. He slammed the hood down, jerked open the front door, and yelled at me, "Get the baby ready! We are going over to Eileen's and Matson's so he can help me fix the car. I knew I shouldn't have sold the other car. You just had to make a trip to Denver to see your mother!"

I stepped over to him. "Just what do you mean, you suppose it's my fault the stupid car has a problem? Just because you sold the other car, doesn't mean you could fix this one. So just button it up."

He glared at me. "You'd better watch your mouth, or I'll slap it shut."

I looked him in the eye. "If I were you, I would be careful how you speak to me. I can talk to Eileen about this. She wasn't really happy with you the last time I talked to her."

He reached over grabbed my arm. "Are you threatening me?"

I could feel the tension in my stomach. I cleared my throat. My voice was shaky - I was scared. I stood my ground. "No, I'm not threatening you, but make no mistake, I am promising you I am not going to take any of your threats."

He seemed surprised - I have never talked to him like that. Usually, I would close down. I decided I was finished. I wasn't going to let him bully me any further. "Let go of my arm right now!"

He released my arm, put his hand on my shoulder,

and whispered in my ear. "I'm sorry. I didn't mean to do that."

I melted on the inside like an ice-cube on a hot summer day. I had no idea I was addicted to his charm. He had the same kind of charming lines, just like my dad. I would not realize the connection until many years later. He wrapped his arms around me, and softly kissed me. His voice was gentle and seductive. "Come on, Sandra, I'll help you get the baby ready to go."

Matson helped Bob fix the car. We had dinner, good conversation, and played cards until midnight.

We spent Christmas and New Years with Eileen and Matson. They were interested in what we were doing, and they loved Cheryl. We talked to Eileen and Matson about us moving to Columbia Villa. They suggested we get in touch with the office at the housing project. Eileen gave Bob the phone number.

In February, 1959, we moved to the housing project. I was delighted! I just knew everything was going to be wonderful! I was in love heaven! Here I was with my little cottage, a girl for me, and I was dreaming about a boy for him. He was happy with his job, his humor was good, and we were in love with each other. Or maybe we were in love with the idea of love.

It was May, and Cheryl's birthday. She would be one-year-old on the sixth. Eileen and Matson were planning a celebration for the event. Eileen was delighted with Cheryl; she was her first grandchild. Eileen baked a chocolate cake with chocolate frosting, decorated it with yellow, red, pink, and white roses. I was impressed - the cake was so gorgeous! I asked Eileen, "How did you learn to do such beautiful art work on this cake?"

She smiled. "Oh, I took a cake decorating class when I was younger. They taught me about the different tips to use, and how to make roses. Thank you for the compliment."

Matson barbecued hamburgers and hot dogs, grilled some corn, and Eileen and I made potato salad and ice tea. We had a wonderful birthday celebration for

Cheryl.

Eileen glanced at Matson. "You know I love these parties, and really enjoy making birthday cakes. By the way, Sandra, when is your birthday?"

I looked at Eileen and said, "Would you believe my birthday is the fifteenth of next month? I would love a cake all decorated. I have never had a birthday cake."

She was puzzled. "What do you mean, you have never had a birthday cake? You're going to be twenty-years-old. What in the world is the matter with your mother?"

I didn't know what to do. My eyes filled with tears, and my voice shook. When I looked at Eileen, she took my hands in hers. "I don't have the words to tell you about my mother. I don't know what the matter with her is. All I know, is that she has never been in her right mind. She lives in a world I know nothing about."

Eileen was concerned. "I didn't mean to pry."

"You didn't. You were just asking a normal question."

It was June. Eileen wanted to know what kind of cake I would like. Chocolate is my favorite. Any color of roses is fine with me. I was excited and overwhelmed, thrilled, and thankful that someone liked me enough to make me a birthday cake. At the same time, I simply didn't know what to do with my feelings, that someone really liked me. I began to wonder, is it really true? I had very few people who had showed me any feelings of tenderness, or caring.

The day came for my birthday, and what a day it was! The cake was beautiful, food was delicious, conversation was delightful, and we played card games until one in the morning. I should have felt warm, accepted, loved, and cared for. I felt none of those things. It seemed like I was another person, standing on the outside of this house, looking in, watching everyone else have a good time. It was like I wasn't really there, only my body. It would be many years later, before I would be able to belong emotionally to anyone or anything.

I loved living at Columbia Villa. We had a small yard, and I treasured the idea that I could take Cheryl outside, put her in her playpen, and mow the grass. Such a small item meant so much to me. It was October,1959, and I discovered I was pregnant.

This is not going to be good. Bob is not going to be happy. He was not overjoyed when I was pregnant with Cheryl. I wonder how I am going to tell him? I know he is fussed up about the fact that he was laid off from his job. This good news is really going to fire him up. I wish I had a way of fixing it. Maybe it's a good thing that I am going to have another baby. I don't want to raise Cheryl as an only child. How do I tell him that Cheryl needs a brother or sister? Of course, I can tell him, that as long as we are together, things will be all right.

Did I know what a lie I was telling myself? Of course not. What we know deep inside ourselves, is far different than what we say on the outside.

I feel nervous, tense, a sense of doom just lurking around the corner. I can feel the tension as he enters the house. I feel like I am walking on egg shells. This is really going to be tricky. I'm glad I fixed his favorite meal of fried chicken, mashed potatoes, gravy, green beans, and vegetable salad, with ice-cream for dessert. And of course, good coffee. The table is set, the aroma of the chicken is breathtaking. I hope I can pull this off.

"What is the big deal? What is going on here? Are we having a party or something?" Bob wanted to know. "It's only Thursday night. What is all of the fuss about?"

I took a deep breath. "Why don't you sit down and eat dinner and I will tell you later."

"No," he replied, "I want to know right now. I can tell something is going on, so spit it out."

My throat was dry; I wasn't sure I could talk. "I'm going to have another baby!" The words just tumbled out of my mouth. Now I was scared.

His face turned red, his eyes looked huge. He raised his voice. "What is wrong with you? What do you mean you are pregnant? What's the matter with you that you would get yourself pregnant?"

Now I was livid, beyond angry! I got in his face

and screamed at him: "What is wrong with you? I can't get pregnant by myself! It takes two to do the tango! Where have you been all your life? You must be dreaming! I have never heard of anything so stupid in all my life! I don't know how anyone can get themselves pregnant!"

He didn't know what to do; he shoved his hands in his pockets, and shook his head. "Well, I guess we'll have another kid, thanks to you."

I turned and glared at him. "I need to go and take care of Cheryl; all this yelling has upset her." I picked her up, took her into the bedroom. I rocked her in my arms, calmed her down, changed her diaper, and got her ready for dinner. I took her out into the kitchen, and placed her in her highchair, then fixed her dinner.

Bob entered the kitchen, sat down at the table to have dinner with us. When he looked over at Cheryl, his face took on a soft glow. He gently said to Cheryl, "How's my little pea picker?"

He slipped into his charm, reached over and took my hand in his. He softly whispered, " I'm so sorry. I don't know what happens to me. I just go off the deep end."

I was putty in his hands.

January, 1960, we are on unemployment, and need to move to a place for less rent. In February, we move to N. Simmons Road, not too far from the Columbia River Slue. Two bedrooms, kitchen, living room. The bathroom is a half-block down a dirt road. There is a public restroom where all the folks who live there share the facility. Okay, I know how this works. I'm been in places like this before.

The kitchen had a wood stove in it. I looked at Bob. "What am I going to do with this stove?"

He glared at me. "You're going to cook on it. The landlady will come over and give you a lesson or two about cooking on a wood stove. I don't know anything about it."

I shrugged my shoulders. "Well, that makes two of us."

Bob went on to tell me that his Uncle Steve also lives here. I have never met him. He let me know I would meet him, and that he doesn't live very far away. He did his best to try and reassure me Uncle Steve would help me with anything I needed.

I looked at Bob, full of questions: "First of all, where are the laundry facilities? How far away does your uncle live?"

Bob took my hand in his. "Come on. I'll take you over to meet my Uncle Steve right now."

We walked the half-block down the dirt road to Steve's house. To my surprise, he was home. Bob introduced us, we shook hands. He was a nice-looking man in his late forties, light brown hair, hazel eyes that twinkled when he smiled. He invited us to come in. We stepped through the door.

Steve gave us a look. "Bob, I haven't seen you since you were fifteen-years-old. I talked to your mother not long ago. I understand you have a baby girl. Where is she?"

'Sandra and I left Cheryl with Eileen and Matson; Eileen is my stepmother," Bob replied.

Steve and Bob's mother, Susie, were brother and sister. Steve was a painter by trade. At this point in time, he was unemployed, due to a back injury. Steve asked Bob how he found out where he lived.

"Well," Bob replied, "I was talking to my mother about the fact we were going to have to move. She suggested that we come out here because she had just talked to you. She said that 'your Uncle Steve lives there and would be delighted to see you, your wife and baby.'"

Steve glanced at Bob. "So, tell me, are you kids going to move to the first cabin that has a for rent sign in the window? That's the one I was telling your mother about."

It's March, and still raining. I'm sick of the rain. I am cold all the time. This wood stove is supposed to keep the house warm. Not for me, it doesn't. Uncle Steve, bless his heart, comes over every morning to build a fire in the wood stove, and gives me a few lessons. One morning he came over and handed me an electric heater.

My eyes filled with tears. Steve placed his arm around my shoulder. He gently said, "Don't cry. I know how hard it is for you to operate that wood stove. I don't know what in the world is the matter with my nephew. I'm going to have a serious talk with him. Here you are pregnant with the second baby. You are still washing diapers for Cheryl. You have to hookup the water hose to the hot water faucet, located next to the bathroom, and then drag one end of the hose to the washing machine in my shed, fill the machine half-full of hot water, and put cold water in, which is in the shed where the washtubs are.

What's the matter with him, that he can't help you with the laundry? Let me get this straight in my mind. I was watching you the other day as you were going through this whole process. First you hook up the water hose, walk half-a-block to my shed, put the hose in the tub, and when it's just about half-full of hot water, walk another half-block to turn the hot water off. Come back, take the hose out of the tub, and put cold water in. By that time, you have already walked a block-and-half, and you haven't even done any laundry. Besides that, it's a wringer washer. Why in the hell can't he do the laundry?"

I wiped my eyes with the hanky Steve handed to me. "You know that Bob is going to think I've talked to you about this situation."

He patted my shoulder, gave me a stern look. "I'll let him know that I have eyes to see with, and what I'm seeing, I don't like. He had better not give you a hard time, or he will have to deal with me."

"Okay," I replied in a shaky voice, "do you know what a hot temper he has?"

He had a sharp edge to his voice. "Oh yes, I've dealt with him when he was a teenager. I thought maybe he might have learned something by this time. I can see he hasn't, and he still thinks someone owes him something. He's still carrying a chip on his shoulder, and daring someone to knock it off. I'm just the guy who can knock it off. You just watch."

I didn't know his uncle knew him so well. I cleared my throat; I wasn't sure if I should tell him about how he looks at other women. I took a deep breath, and decided I might just as well tell him a few other things about the situation. Well here goes: "When we are in the car, and Bob sees a woman crossing the street or walking along the sidewalk, he certainly has some things to say about women."

"Like what?" Steve wanted to know.

"I'm embarrassed to tell you."

Steve quietly said, "Just remember - I've known Bob for a long time. I wouldn't be surprised at anything he would say or do."

I looked at the floor. I couldn't bring myself to look at Steve.

"He looks at their boobs, and he says things like, "Just look at those knockers on that broad!" He looks at their bottoms, and remarks, "Just look at the way she swings her butt. I wonder how good she is in bed?"

"Oh," he replied. "I've heard him say those same things, when he was a teenager. I want you to let me take care of things "

I put my hand to my lips. "Okay," I said, with a lot more confidence than I felt.

After Steve left, I sat down at the kitchen table. I put my head in my hands. I felt a heaviness deep inside that I had never felt before. There are many things I could not tell Steve, things I can barely say to myself on the inside.

I began to turn things over in my mind, and wonder what in the world is wrong with me, never realizing that some of the problems belonged to Bob. It takes two to have a problem. How in the world could I bring myself to tell him, that many times Bob acts like he is going to make love to me, and then turns over and masturbates? A sense of shame washed over me. This is something I will never be able to talk about. I have to keep it hidden deep within. Somehow, when I say something to Bob about it, he says it's because I have no sex appeal. I don't know what that is. I'm only twenty-years old. I was only sixteen when I married him. How am I supposed to know what sex appeal is?

Once again, I began to realize that it's just a matter of time before this whole thing will be over. How long will it be, before it's really over?

The tears were rolling down my cheeks when I heard Cheryl stirring in her crib.

I don't know when Steve talked to Bob or what was said. The following day, I was putting the laundry in the basket to take down to the shed to wash. Bob stepped over to me, and placed his arm around me. He pulled me to him. "I'll do the laundry today. What do I do first?"

I explained to Bob that the clothes in the basket were already divided. "The white and light-colored clothes are on top, the colored clothes are on the bottom. When you come back from washing the clothes, and hanging them on the close-line, I'll have the diapers ready that are in the diaper pail."

Bob wanted to know why he couldn't take all the laundry at the same time.

"Well," I said, "it's like this: the diapers have been soaking in bleach water. I wash the regular clothes first. Then I empty the washing machine, put in fresh water, then wash the diapers and Cheryl's clothes. I put Cheryl's clothes in a separate container. Before I wash the diapers, I dump the water out that the diapers have been soaking in, rinse the diapers; then they are ready to wash.

He gave me a sharp stare. "That's a lot of damn work, just to do the laundry. I sure could think of an easier way of doing it, if I were you."

I turned and glared at him. I could hardly believe what I was hearing. "Of course, you could find an easier way of doing things! You are never here to help with anything. You are very good at finding fault. Trouble is, you don't have any faults, everybody else does. You may not always be right, but you are never wrong. You are so good, that whoever you are working for won't pay you what you think you are worth. You could make a lot of money, if someone would just buy you for what you are worth! Then we could sell you, for what you think you are worth, and be millionaires!"

He was angry. I've never talked to him like that before. I was shaking inside like a bowl-full of jello. He stepped over to me, grabbed my arm, and snarled when he said, "I oughta' slap you into the middle of next week!"

I took a deep breath. "Well, you can, if that will make you feel better. Just help yourself." I could tell that took him by surprise. He simply didn't know what to do. He left to do the laundry.

After Bob left, I discovered I had just learned something important, something I could use later, to be of benefit to me. I could bully him by agreeing with him. Now, I decided, I was one up on him.

When Bob returned from doing the laundry, he was apologetic, warm, and tender. He never said a word about the laundry, and I didn't ask.

Cheryl had her second birthday. We celebrated it at Eileen's and Matson's house. We had a wonderful time. Eileen was curious. "Sandra, who is going to take care of Cheryl when you go to have the baby?"

"Well," I replied, "I've been talking to my sister, Karen. She lives in Denver, and will be coming in June to stay with us. She said she would stay for a couple of months."

Bob gave me a look of surprise. "I didn't know about Karen coming! How come you didn't tell me about it?"

I placed my hand on his arm, and quietly said, "I can't tell you if you're not at home."

Karen arrived at the end of June. I was so glad to see her. I had just had my twenty-first birthday, and Karen had just had her seventeenth birthday. My birthday is the fifteenth of June, her's is the fourteenth.

Debbie arrived the 20th of July. Bob left to go to work, while I had the baby. He took the baby and me home three days later. Bob and his mother went fishing the day I came home with the new baby. I could tell they showed no interest in the new arrival.

Karen and I looked at each other, shrugged our shoulders. "Well, so much for that. I guess they weren't too interested. Maybe they will have some luck fishing. However, I think they probably went to the nearest tavern. Bob's mother always says she's going fishing when she wants to go out drinking."

Bob showed up at three a.m. I was feeding our new baby, Debbie. Bob came over and stood by the rocking chair, patting me on the head.

"I'm sorry I was gone so long. My mother wasn't ready to leave. I couldn't just leave her there. I was her ride home."

I rocked Debbie back-and-forth in the rocker. "Uh huh," I replied. " I know she has never left the house and gone to the tavern by herself, without a ride. It's too bad that she needs an escort at her age. She is way past the age of twenty-one. I just know your stepdad, Maynard, was worried sick about where Susie was. She has never been out this late before. I'm sure he was pacing the floor."

I could tell he was getting a little angry. His body stiffened, he gave me a nasty stare. "I'm going to bed. I've had enough of this conversation. So, what if I wasn't here to coo over this new baby? I wasn't happy about having another brat in the first place."

I could feel the hot tears roll down my face. Fear gripped me on the inside like a vice. I have felt this way many times before.

Once again, I began to know deep inside, that I would have to leave again. Maybe this time, it would be for good. I didn't know when or how, but I knew it was going to happen.

10

He was sweet and kind, when he got up in the morning. He had slipped his jacket of charm on. He was good with his words of 'I'm so sorry, I just don't know what came over me yesterday. I know I shouldn't have left you alone with the new baby." Of course, it worked! I melted into his arms when he wrapped them around me, and whispered in my ear, "Baby Doll, I love you so much! I can't live without you. You are my whole world."

I was sucked into the whirlpool one more time. He stayed sweet and kind, and was helping with the chores at home, looking for a job, playing with Cheryl. and paying attention to the new baby. What more could I ask for?

Karen went back to Denver, at the end of August. She needed to look for a job, and a place to live. She didn't want to stay with Mother, and Harry, our stepdad. Before she left, she wanted me to know that if I needed anything, to be sure and let her know. She knew things were not good between Bob and I, no matter how the pretense was at the moment. Of course, what we know on the inside is far different than what we are willing to admit on the outside. I didn't know then, that many of us live in a world of great pretenders.

After Karen left, things began to fall apart once again. Bob began to drink more and more, and came home later and later each night. Always wanting to argue. I kept asking him when he was going to find a job. He had a ton of excuses. "They don't pay enough for my skill level." "I don't like that kind of work." "I didn't like the setup." "The guy who was doing the hiring had a nasty attitude." "I liked the place I went to last week; the guy I talked to said he would call me this week."

Of course, that never happened. He started getting so he would twist my arm, or slap me on the back. I began to feel frightened. Once again, I knew it was time to go. I made some phone calls while he was out looking for a job. I made arrangements to go to the Volunteers of America Mothers' and Childrens' home. The plan was in place - all I needed was a day I knew he would be gone.

A few days later, I was in the shed doing laundry. I stepped into Steve's cabin to talk to him about my plan. He knew things were not good with his nephew, Bob.

"Where are you, Steve?" I yelled.

"In the kitchen," he replied.

I glanced at Steve. "I need your help. I need a ride to the Volunteers of America Mothers' and Childrens' Home. I don't want Bob to know where I am. Can you help me out?"

He shifted his weight from one foot to the other. "When are you planning on leaving?"

"In the morning," I replied. "Bob is going to the coast to look for work, which doesn't make much sense to me. If there's no work in Portland, what makes him think there is work at the coast? What do I know? I'm just his wife. Okay, here's the plan: as soon as Bob leaves I'll get the kids and my clothes packed in suitcases. I'll call you when I'm ready to go. All you have to do, is come and pick us up. Bob said he won't be back for a couple of days. He's going to stay with Eileen and Matson, in Coos Bay. They moved a couple of months ago."

Steve said, "Give me a call in the morning, to let me know how things are working out. If you haven't called by noon, I'll know he hasn't gone, and things aren't working as planned."

I called Steve the following morning at ten o'clock. He came at ten-thirty to take us where we were going. I called Steve after we were settled into our new location. While I was talking to Steve, he told me that Bob had returned from the coast. "He's heartbroken that you and the children are gone."

I asked Steve if Bob had found a job. I heard him as he cleared his throat. "Well, no, he hasn't. Bob told me he's been so upset since you and the kids left, that he's not able to even think about looking for a job. I have never seen him cry, like I saw him cry yesterday. I think he's really sorry for everything he's done and said. Sandra, he wants you to call him. Maybe he really is sorry. Can you give him another chance?"

I was scared. I knew I really loved Bob, and I missed him. I was homesick, and I wanted to see him. I told Steve I would call Bob the following day.

Of course, the more I thought about Bob and the way he could be so tender and kind, and whisper sweet things in my ear, the more I missed him. I knew the second I would hear his voice on the phone, I would melt inside. Why is this so hard? Maybe he's really sorry. Maybe all of this is my fault, and maybe it isn't. I sure don't know what the answer is. I just know that when I decided to leave and take the children with me, it seemed so clear at the time. Right now, I want to talk to him and hear his voice.

I tossed and turned in my bed. I was restless, my stomach felt tight, and I was scared. I paced the floor several times during the night. The children slept peacefully in their beds, as I kept turning thoughts over and over in my mind. As the sun rose, and a new day was dawning, the world kept turning no matter what kind of problem I was dealing with.

He must have been sitting on top of the phone. It only rang once. I heard the excitement in his voice. "Hello?" he said.

My heart was beating a hundred-miles-a-minute, my throat was dry, my hands shook. I finally managed to say, "Bob, can you come and take us home?"

"Of course, I can," he replied. I heard the break in his voice. I knew he was close to tears. "You can't imagine how much I have missed you and the children. All I want is my wife and my children."

"Okay," I replied, "the children and I will be ready in an hour." I was excited that we were going to the home I missed. At the same time, I was scared.

What if he acts up again? Goes out drinking, comes home late at night wanting to start a fight? I guess I will have to deal with that later. He sounded so honest and heartbroken. Just remember, you have been down this road before. He sounds good for a few days. Time will tell.

11

Cheryl screeched and yelled when she saw her daddy. She was excited to be in his arms. He put his arm around me, and kissed me. He whispered in my ear, "I'm so sorry. I'll be better. I'll find a job, I promise, even if I have to go to work at the coast. I know this has been really hard on you. I know I have to grow up, be a man, and take care of things. My Uncle Steve has been laying the law down to me. I know what he's telling me, is right. I haven't been doing my share. I've bullied you with my temper. I'm really sorry. I know that I've been in the wrong."

I believed him. I'm sure that he was telling the truth. At the same time he was saying those words, I was putty in his hands. I was on cloud nine, as we rode home in the car. His promises didn't last long. A few nights later, he came home drunk. He had been out with his mother. He was in a foul mood when he came home. It was ten o'clock the; children were in bed asleep.

He started his yelling, "What the hell is the matter with you? This house is a mess! The dishes are still in the sink, clothes are on the couch, shoes laying on the floor, dust on the window sill,
windows need to be washed. You are a lousy housekeeper, you can't take care of anything! No other man in this world would be attracted to you, much less take care of you. I'm doing you a favor by staying with you."

I was in a state of shock. I didn't know what to say or do. I just stared at him as if I didn't know who he was.

He screamed, "What in the hell are you staring at?"

I was frozen - I couldn't answer. I felt like my legs were made of paper, nothing seemed to make sense. I slowly got up from the chair and walked as if I was dreaming. I went into the bedroom, shut the door, undressed, put my nightgown on, and went to bed.

The following morning, I got the children up, fixed their breakfast, got them ready for the day. Bob was sleeping on the couch. I pretended like he was not at home. I was past being angry. I was in a rage. I wanted to be rid of him forever.

A few nights later, he was out drinking again. He came home at three in the morning, yelling what a rotten life he had living with me. He placed his hands on my upper arms, gave me a shove. I was stunned! He's never done that before. He grabbed my arm and twisted it. I yelled, "Let me go! Let me go!" He finally did. He was still screaming. I ran into the bedroom and shut the door. I called the operator, and told her I needed the police immediately. She could hear Bob screaming in the other room. She assured me they would be there immediately - "Do not hang up!" (in 1960 there was no 911; it didn't exist).

Six policemen showed up. They could hear him screaming, as they approached the door. They came through the door, yelling, "Quiet down! This is the police department! If you don't, you will be placed under arrest."

He shut up immediately.

A large policeman stepped forward. He looked to be about six-foot-six, shoulders like a football player. He glared at Bob. "What's the matter with you, that you have to yell at your wife?"

Bob's face turned red. He sneered at the officer. "Just look at her - she's a mess, no sex appeal, lousy housekeeper. Always nagging at me because I don't have a job. I can't find the kind of job I want. They don't pay me what I'm worth."

The officer looked him in the eye. "Really?" he replied. The officer stepped forward, a little closer to Bob. "What makes you so special? Do you have a college degree, lots of job skills, good communication skills, good job record?"

I could see that Bob was stunned. It was as if someone had let the air out of his balloon. He shrank from the officer. His voice became softer. He seemed to be a little bit scared. He shrugged his shoulders. He said, "I think I'll go to bed." Bob stepped into the bedroom and closed the door.

The officer walked over to me; I could tell he was concerned for my safety. "You know his behavior is only going to get worse. You need to take some steps to protect yourself. If he ever comes home again drunk like he was tonight, if you had a gun, you could shoot him. Make sure he falls into the house. You could claim he was a burglar."

I sat in the rocking chair for a long time, after the police left.

I began to wonder how it would work, to shoot him. I would have to make sure I killed him. It began to sound like it might be a good plan. I sure would be rid of him for good. I'll go over to Steve's sometime later today, and ask him if I can borrow his gun. Right now, I need to go to bed and get some sleep. I seem to be exhausted.

I was surprised that all the racket didn't wake the children. They slept right through everything. It was four-thirty. I was hoping the children would at least sleep until eight o'clock. The children did sleep until eight. I got them up, dressed them for the day, fixed breakfast for us, left Bob sleeping in the bedroom. After breakfast, I put Debbie in the stroller. Cheryl walked along beside me, as we made our way over to Steve's cabin. I knocked on his door. He yelled, "Come in! What brings you and the children out so early?"

I took a deep breath. "You know, if I had a good cup of coffee, and a cigarette, I could tell you all about the events that took place last night."

He poured me a cup of coffee, handed me a cigarette. I lit it, took a deep drag, blew out the smoke, as if I was gathering my thoughts.

"It was three in the morning, when Bob came home last night. He was drunk, yelling about what a rotten wife I am, gave me a shove, twisted my arm. I managed to get away from him, ran into the bedroom, and called the police. They showed up in a few minutes. They let Bob know that he could either quiet down, or go to jail. He shut up and went to bed. One of the policemen suggested to me, that if I had a gun, I could shoot him, as long as I thought he was a burglar, and fell into the house - 'Make sure that you kill him.' Could I borrow your gun?"

Steve looked at me, as if he couldn't believe what he had just heard. "Let me get this straight - you want me to loan you my gun, so that you can shoot my nephew? Not in a million years would I do anything like that! If you are planning on leaving him again, I can help you do that. I will not help you kill him. That's crazy thinking! You wouldn't get away with it. What would your children do without their dad? And you would probably be in prison."

I didn't know what to say to Steve. I felt like I was a different person. Like I had just slipped into a different personality. I have never talked like this before. It seemed like a trance. A world I knew nothing about. I was not a violent person. I could feel myself on the edge of insanity.

I excused myself, took the children home. Bob was up when we got there. He came over to me, placed his arm around my shoulder. "I'm sorry about what happened last night. I don't know what happens to me, at times like that."

I just stared at him. I knew I didn't want to talk to him. I just shrugged my shoulders, turned around, and made a pot of coffee, scrambled some eggs, made some toast, and left the room. I felt empty inside, drained of all emotion. I went through the motions of sorting the laundry, making the beds, dusting the furniture.

12

Bob had finished his breakfast. He was sitting at the table drinking coffee, smoking a cigarette. He looked up at me, cleared his throat, and said very softly, "I'll watch the children if you want to do laundry."

I gave him a blank stare, shrugged my shoulders. "Suit yourself," I said with a flat tone. I simply didn't care if he took care of the kids or not. He sure wasn't interested yesterday, so what's the big deal today? I picked up the laundry, and walked out of the house. I went over to Steve's and did laundry.

By the time I finished, the children were taking a nap. Bob was looking at the employment section of the newspaper. He looked up, as I came through the door with the empty clothes basket.

"You know what?" he said with an excited tone in his voice. "According to this ad in the paper, they are hiring at the lumber mill in Coos Bay. It will be worth it for me to go to Coos Bay on Sunday. I can stay with Eileen and Matson. I'll call you on Monday, to let you know if I find a job. Then I'll come and get you and the children. I know you'll like it in Coos Bay."

I moved like a robot. I felt like I had no emotion left. I knew I wasn't going to move to Coos Bay, or any place else with Bob. I had made up my mind that as soon as he left, I would pack the suitcases and the children, and be gone to Denver. He could come back whenever he damn well wanted to. I was finished. Last night was the last straw.

All of a sudden, he stopped talking. He looked at me like he was seeing me for the first time. "What's the matter with you? You haven't said a word. Don't you want to move to Coos Bay? Answer me."

I could feel my eyes burning. I didn't want him to know how bad I was feeling. I folded my arms in front of me. "I'll go wherever you want me to go." I knew the second I said it, I didn't mean a word of it.

I could tell he was getting agitated. His tone

became sharp. "I'm going out for a while." He slammed the door when he left.

Well, isn't that just ducky. He'll probably come back drunk. If he does, I wonder if I could tie him to the bed with a long rope? Funny thing is, I probably don't know how to tie a hard-enough knot. If he were to fall in bed in a drunken stupor, he would probably wake up and yell, "What the hell are you doing?" How would I tell him that I was planning on beating him to death with a two-by-four, or a hammer? What would I do with the body? Besides that, there would be a lot of blood. One thing for sure - I would be rid of him for good. I like that idea.

I rose from my chair, took the children into the bedroom, and got them ready for bed. I looked at the kids' innocent faces. Tears filled my eyes.

How in the world could I kill their dad? They would be left with no parents. I would go to prison, for the rest of my life. Sandra, you had better decide that you are leaving him, and take the children to Denver with you. Call your sister, Karen. You know she will send you the tickets.

He came home about three a.m., in a pleasant mood for a change. He gently shook me, whispered in my ear, "Sweetheart, I want to talk to you for a few minutes."

I turned over and stretched, as if I had been asleep. Squinted my eyes at him. He wrapped his arms around me. "I'm so sorry that I was crabby with you earlier. I know I can be hard to live with at times. I talked to Eileen on the phone, and she said to come on down to Coos Bay – 'I'm sure you'll find a job. I'd love to have you and Sandra and the children close by'."

I kissed him, and told him everything would be okay, as long as we had each other. I also knew that as soon as he left on Sunday, I would call my sister, Karen, and have her send me the tickets. The children and I would be gone when he came back from the coast.

I could pretend. I was good at it. I did a lot of pretending when I was a kid. I haven't forgotten how to act, that everything is great. What I didn't know, was when you try to fool yourself, you will pay a very high price.

I prepared breakfast in the morning. Coffee,

French-toast, sausage. He was impressed. He wanted to know, "What's the big deal? I'm only going to Coos Bay, to see if I get a job."

I smiled sweetly at him. "Oh, I just wanted you to have a good breakfast before you left on your new adventure. It might be a while before you eat again."

He patted my shoulder. "Thank you for thinking of me. I had better put some clothes in a suitcase. I'll probably be gone for a while. At least a week or two."

My body tensed up, my stomach was tight, my throat was dry. My voice was squeaky. "Take as long as you need to. The children and I will be okay. We'll be here when you get back." I could feel my insides shaking. I knew we would be gone.

Part of me felt powerful, another part of me was scared. Scared of what he was going to say or do, when he gets back and finds us gone. I'll think about that when the time comes. Right now, I have to be smooth as glass.

He left at noon. I began to plan what to take, and what to leave behind. I knew that the only items we would be taking, would be our clothes. I called Karen. I told her of my plans, and she said she would have the tickets to me on Tuesday. This was Sunday. I had two days to get things ready and packed. I felt empty inside. I moved like a person in a trance. I knew I couldn't live with him, and I didn't know how I was going to live without him. I could feel the rage that was inside me, like a boiling pot of water. I didn't know about the hurt and pain that I carried inside of me, and I had no idea about the hurt and pain that we were giving to each other.

Deep inside me, I wanted revenge. I would not discover until years later, that revenge only takes place in the halls of your mind. To hold a grudge, will never bring freedom. Only forgiveness brings peace of mind.

There was a part of me that knew I would love him forever; he was the father of my children. At this point in time, I had no idea about feelings. I didn't know what I felt. The only feeling I knew about, was anger.

13

For the next two days, I washed clothes, packed suitcases, packed boxes that contained dishes, linens, towels, and household supplies. I put all those items in the shed, locked it up with a padlock, and took the key with me. Steve took me to the airport, on Tuesday morning. The children and I boarded the plane for Denver, Colorado.

As I sat in the seat with the children, I felt like a stranger to myself, as if I didn't know what I was doing, where I was, or where I was going. I was just a person on a plane, in a seat, with a couple of kids. Going where the plane was taking us. I felt like I was dreaming.

Karen was at the airport, ready to take us to her apartment. She lived across the street from our mother, and Harry. I was glad to see her, and at the same time, I was at loose ends with myself. I was quietly brooding. I knew inside myself that I had to leave him. As we rode along in the taxi, I wondered what was going to take place.

I don't feel right inside. I can't talk to anyone about the fact that I love Bob. How can I make them understand, that I believe I have enough love for both of us? I could help him if he would let me. All he needs is the love of a good woman, and he would be different.

"Sandra," my sister shook me, "are you sleeping?"

"Oh, no," I replied. 'I was just thinking about how I wished things would have turned out."

Karen gave me a puzzled look. "Well, you know this isn't happy-ever-after. This is real life."

Why don't you just pretend that you are here for an extended vacation, get a job, a place of your own, and everything will be fine? You are good at pretending - you have done it for years. Then, when Bob shows up to take you home after your vacation, both of you will be glad to see each other. We'll just keep pretending it will work. You know he is going to be mad as hell, when he discovers that you and the children are gone. Not only that, he is going to be upset that you have locked up all the household items. Maybe he will get the idea that he has made you very angry, and you are just paying him back. Never mind worrying about this stuff now. I'll think about it when I see him again.

  Mother came over the following morning. I could tell she was upset. She looked at me with one of her wild stares. Her eyes were glassy and huge. They looked like they were too big for her face. She began to scream, "What's going on? I'm going to get blamed, because you've left Bob!"

  I walked over to my mother, took her hands in mine. "Calm down, Mother. I'll take care of it. This has nothing to do with you. This is between Bob and me."

  She settled down a bit, lowered her voice. "I don't want him blaming me for anything. I don't want him in my house. I won't be able to stand it. I can't fix it. What am I going to do?"

  I looked her in the eye, and calmly said, "Your job is to be the childrens' grandma. My job is to take care of my own problems."

  "Okay," she replied. "I guess you know what you're doing." She headed for the door, and went home.

  I went to work where my sister was employed. Karen worked the early shift, and I worked the later one.

  I decided I needed a boyfriend. I found a friend. His name was Shorty. What was I thinking? I wasn't. The only thoughts I had, were that I was going to pay Bob back for all the names he ever called me, and all the times he went out and got drunk.

  It was the middle of October, on a Saturday afternoon. Shorty was in the living room, when a loud knock was heard. I opened the door - Bob stood on the stair. I was startled, didn't know what to say. I was scared, my insides began to shake. I knew my voice was going to be shaky. My mouth and throat became as dry as the sands on a desert.

  "What are you doing here?" I wanted to know.

  His eyes filled with tears. "I've come to take you and the children home with me."

  I took a step back into the room. Shorty was sitting on the couch. Bob looked at him with a cold stare.

Shorty stepped forward, put out his hand, and shook Bob's, as he said, "Hi, my name is Shorty." He was a short man, about five-feet-eight-inches in height. Light brown hair with a golden cast to it. Soft brown eyes, his voice was soft, and his manner was gentle.

Bob's voice was gruff. "What are you doing here with my wife?"

I could tell Shorty was startled. He cleared his throat. "Sandra and I are friends, nothing more. We were having a nice chat." Shorty stepped over to me, took my hand in his. His voice was soft. "I'll see you again. It was nice talking to you. We will talk again, in the near future."

Bob glared at him, as he went out the door.

Bob came over to me, put his arm around me, bowed his head. I could see the tears roll down his cheeks. He looked at me. "I'm so sorry for the way I've treated you. You have no idea how much I've missed you and the children. I had a talk with my Uncle Steve. He informed me that he didn't blame you for leaving me. I had to admit that I didn't treat you right. I'll make it up to you. Will you please come back to me?"

"Bob," I replied, "that will take some serious thinking."

Of course, Bob had no idea that Shorty and I were discussing the situation, when he knocked at the door. I was not about to tell him that I wanted to pay him back for the way he had been treating me.

Bob wiped the tears from his eyes. He wrapped his arms around me, and softly kissed me. He placed his hands on my shoulders, looked at me with his soft brown eyes, and gently said in a soft voice, "Can I spend the night?"

I could feel my insides turning to jelly. One part of me wanted him to stay, another part of me wanted to be strong. I took a deep breath. I could feel the lump in my throat; I knew my voice was
going to be shaky. I cleared my throat. "You know, I need to do some serious thinking. For you to spend the night would not be a good idea. I need some time and

space to think through what I'm going to do."

I could tell he didn't like the answer he received. He placed his hands in his pockets, and slowly walked away. "I'll see you in a couple of days. If you need anything, you can call me. I've been staying over at Cindy's place."

I didn't bother to ask him, how long he had been in town. I didn't want to know.

A few days later, he came to the house, knocked at the door, came into the kitchen, sat down at the table, and took out a bottle of pills. "Okay," he said, "this is it. I'm going to kill myself. I'm going to take these pain pills that belong to Rose."

I looked at him. I felt like this was a scene from a movie. "Okay," I replied, "I'll get you a glass of water."

In just a few minutes, his face turned pale, his eyes took on a glaze that I've never seen before. I knew something was really wrong. I ran to the phone booth on the corner.

I dialed the operator. I was terrified. I screamed, "Send the police! My husband is dying! He took some pain pills! I don't know what they are! He looks awful! Hurry as fast as you can!"

"Okay," the operator replied. " Slow down and tell me your address." My body was shaking like a leaf in a windstorm.

"My address? You want my address? It's 2710 West Ada."

I ran back to the apartment. I could see the police car coming down the street. I waved my arms at them. The car pulled to the curb. I was yelling, "Come quick! He's in here!"

Bob turned and yelled at me. "You bitch! I'm not going to the hospital. I'm going to die right here!"

The policemen took him by the arm, one on each side. They walked him outside to the car. Bob kept yelling, "I wanna' die inside that bitch's apartment."

The officer looked him in the eye. "Get in the car right now. You can die in there."

They put him in the back seat of the patrol car, the officers in the front seat. They turned on their siren, signaled to me to come over to the car. The officer said, "We will be taking him to Denver General Hospital. You can check on him tomorrow."

I went to the hospital, the following day. They had pumped his stomach as soon as he arrived. He was in the mental health ward. I asked the nurse why he was placed there. She informed me that any time they receive a patient who has attempted suicide, they keep them for a six-week evaluation. I asked if I could see him, and the nurse told me what room he was in.

I found him in a private room, in a hospital bed, both side-rails up. He was not allowed out of bed by himself, until the following morning. He looked like a little boy, waiting for his mother to come and get him.

I could feel the tears in my eyes; he looked so sad and bewildered. I was at a loss for words. I walked around the bed, put my hands on the side-rail. I softly asked him, "How are you feeling today?"

"I'm not sure," he replied, "but I'll tell you one thing. I only did it because of you."

Those words hung in the air like rocks that had been shot from an explosion.

I simply walked away. I had no words that I could say. I was shocked. I felt like a zombie. I went back to see him, a few days later. He seemed more at ease. He was up walking around, and greeted me with a smile, put his arm around me, and kissed me on the cheek.

We sat down at a table, he took my hand in his, his eyes were soft, his voice gentle. "How are the kids? You know I miss you and the children. I hope I can come home when I'm released from the hospital."

I didn't know what to say. I felt uncomfortable inside. I took a deep breath. All of a sudden, I felt scared. Part of me wanted to take him in my arms, and tell him how much I loved him. Another part of me wanted him to stay away, but not too far away.

Instead of telling him no, you can't come home

until we can see a counselor, I said, "That would be nice, but not right now." I seemed to be made of jello on the inside. I didn't know at the time, that I needed to get acquainted with my insides. I was living on 'No Think Ave.', with a cross-street of 'I'm Sorry'.

14

Bob was released from the hospital, and went back to stay with my friend, Cindy, and her mother, Rose. Bob was wanting us to get a place of our own. I was enjoying my freedom. I liked hanging out with my friend, Shorty. Bob was furious about the situation. It seemed to be okay if he hung out with Cindy. He could hang out with whoever he wanted to, but I couldn't. We were at odds with one another.

It was a cold, rainy and wet Saturday afternoon, a good day for a pot of soup. Karen opened the door, came into the kitchen. "What are you cooking that smells so good?" she wanted to know.

"I'm cooking some soup," I replied.

She took a deep whiff. "Boy, that smells good. "What did you put in it?"

"I started with a couple of cans of tomatoes, onions, green pepper, carrots, potatoes, corn, hamburger, garlic powder, salt, pepper, and Italian spices. Oh, yes, and a hand-full of macaroni. The biscuits will be ready in fifteen minutes - I just put them in the oven to bake.

It was midnight. We were in bed sound asleep. There was a loud knock at the door. I sat up in bed, fully awake. I heard Bob yelling. "Open this door, and do it right now or I will break it down!"

I could tell by the tone of his voice, and the slur of his words, that he was rip-roaring drunk. He didn't wait for me to open the door. He hit the door with his shoulder, and came rushing into the house. The door was old, so it didn't take much to break.

"Where in the hell is he? I know he's here! I saw his car this afternoon!"

I stared at him, my mouth open, my heart racing. "What are you talking about? Who are you looking for?"

He glared at me. "That stupid Shorty, he's here, I know it." He looked in all the rooms and decided he wasn't there. "It's a good thing he's not here. I would've killed him, and you with him."

The landlady was at the door; she looked around, and I could tell by the look on her face she was furious. "What happened here? Look at this door! Who did this?"

I pointed to Bob. "He did," I replied.

She got up close to his face, shook her finger at him, and with a nasty tone to her voice, she told him to go. "If I ever see you around here again, I'll call the police and have you hauled off as a trespasser."

He got in his car, slammed the door, and screeched his tires, as he went around the corner.

The following day, the landlady came down to our apartment to pay us a visit. It was not a friendly one. She informed us that she wanted us to move. She was not going to put up with having her door busted in. She gave us thirty-days to find a new residence.

Two weeks later we moved to a two-bedroom basement apartment.

Bob wanted to come back home. He promised he would be different. All he wanted was his wife and his children. If I would just give him another chance, I would see that he was different.

I was enjoying my freedom. I didn't want him to come back home. I was having fun, hanging out with Shorty.

We had been in our new apartment for two weeks. Bob showed up one morning. I could tell by the way he looked, that he was planning something. I felt scared, a foreboding fear that startled me. He stared at me with a look that I had never seen before. His eyes were wild, they had a dark cast to them. He rose from the chair he had been sitting in at the kitchen table, walked over to the sink, opened the silverware drawer and took out a butcher knife.

I was terrified! My legs were shaking, my whole body felt like a leaf in a windstorm. I raised my voice, "What are you going to do with that knife?"

He stepped over to me, and backed me up to the screen door. He pointed the knife at me. "I'm going to kill you."

I looked at him as calmly as I could. "Okay," I

replied. "I'm ready."

He didn't know what to do. He looked at me as if I had shocked him with an electric current. He put the knife down, turned to me with his sad brown eyes that were filled with tears. His voice was shaky. "I'm going to kill myself instead."

I looked at him and replied, "I think that's a better idea."

He walked out the door.

It took a long time for me to calm myself down. I felt like my whole body had been in a tornado.

Thanksgiving, Christmas, and New Years' came and went with no trauma. Bob came every now and then. He seemed to be calmer, and appeared to be resigned to the fact, that maybe I wouldn't take him back.

It was the middle of January. The day was cold, snowing outside, wind was blowing, a good day to stay indoors. There was a loud rap at the door. Bob stepped into the kitchen. He looked cold, his face was red. He shook the snow from his jacket and brushed the flakes from his hair. I offered him a cup of coffee. He looked at me with his soft brown eyes. I found myself looking into his eyes, like I had never seen them before. For some reason, they looked different. His voice was gentle.

"May I have a cup of coffee? I'm so cold."

"Of course, you can," I replied.

I was longing to wrap my arms around him. I wanted him to stay. At that moment in time, I wanted to tell him how much I loved him, that I was sorry for the way things had turned out. Maybe we could start again.

Cheryl came into the kitchen. She was so happy to see her daddy. She squealed, "Daddy! Daddy!" He lifted her up into his lap. She wrapped her little arms around him, hugged him and hugged him. My eyes filled with tears, I didn't trust my voice to speak. I could see that he was the love of my little girl's life.

I cleared my throat, shifted my weight from one foot to the other, folded my arms across my chest. "So, what brings you out on such a nasty, cold winter day like today?"

He looked up at me. "I'm going out to look for a job, and I thought perhaps you would like to go along."

"Well," I replied, "I don't know what I would do with the children - it's such a nasty day outside."

My sister Karen, God bless her heart, stepped into the kitchen, poured herself a cup of coffee, sat down at the table. She put both her hands around her cup, took a sip of coffee. "I'm not doing anything important today. You can leave them here with me, if you want to."

I left with Bob. I didn't have a clue where he was going, and I didn't ask. All of a sudden, we were at Denver General Hospital, in the parking lot. I looked at Bob. I was confused, and didn't know what in the world we were doing at the hospital.

"What are we doing at the hospital? I'm not looking for a job at this place."

He raised his voice, looked at me sharply. "Because you are crazy, and you need a doctor to talk to. Your appointment is at eleven. It's ten forty-five right now."

"Okay," I replied."

We went inside the building, I took a seat, he went to the appointment desk.

I decided that I would fix him! Every question the doctor asks me, I'll give the opposite answer. Just watch this. All of a sudden, I began to laugh. Bob looked at me. I could tell my laughter was getting to him.

"What the hell is so funny?" he wanted to know.

I kept laughing. "I'm crazy! I'm crazy! I'm happy I've found out what's wrong with me! I'm so happy!"

The nurse came and called my name. Bob got up to go with me. The nurse shook her head and told him no.

"The doctor wants to see Sandra first, then he will talk to you."

The doctor talked to me for about fifteen minutes, asked me a lot of questions. I gave him the opposite answer to every question. When he ended the interview, I went out to the waiting room.

Bob went in to see the doctor. When he came back to the waiting room, I could tell the session didn't go very well. He grabbed my hand, pulled me to my feet, gave me one of his stern looks. His voice was gruff and low. "Hurry up, let's get out of here."

We got in the car. He started the engine. He was in a hurry, ticked off he couldn't go fast because the streets were slick. He was quiet on the way home. His face was red, his knuckles were white as he gripped the steering wheel.

I hung onto my side of the car. I wasn't sure I was going to get home in one piece. I also knew to stay quiet. I could feel my heart pounding, my breathing was shallow. I was relieved when he pulled up in front of the house. The second the car stopped, I had the door open and was out on the street. I slammed the door, headed for the house, and never looked back. I could hear the brakes screeching as he went around the corner.

Karen looked at me as I came through the door. "What in the world happened? You're as white as a sheet!"

"Let me sit down, and I'll tell you about it. First of all, he took me to Denver General Hospital. He decided I was crazy, and needed to see a doctor. He had made an appointment that I knew nothing about. I thought it was funny, and I laughed and laughed. He didn't think it was a laughing matter. I went in to see the doctor, and gave him all the wrong answers. After the appointment, Bob was so mad I just knew I wasn't going to make it home in one piece. The streets were slick and icy, and we slid from one side of the street to the other. I was thankful there wasn't much traffic or we could have had a serious accident."

"You know, Karen, just this morning, when Bob came to the house, I was thinking that maybe we could get back together. I love him, and maybe I could make him happy. Maybe, just maybe, I wasn't as good as I could have been. I would like to give it another try. But not today. Maybe in a couple of weeks."

Karen folded her arms, cleared her throat, gave me a serious look. "Well, Sandra, I've been thinking about getting a place of my own. I've had a hunch that you might be thinking about giving it another try. I really hope it works out for the best."

Karen moved. Bob wanted to move in with me and the children. I wanted him back, and I didn't want it to be the way it was before. I didn't know how I was going to make things different. I knew how to argue with him, what made him angry, and what buttons to push. I didn't know his heart, and he didn't know mine. Bob and I did the dance of anger together. We simply didn't know any different.

It was the middle of March. Bob moved back home with me. By the middle of May, I knew I was pregnant with our third baby. By the end of May, he was gone again. June came, and I celebrated my birthday with my sister, Karen, and the children. I was twenty-two, two children and another one on the way.

I had no money. I applied for Aid to Dependent Children. The State of Colorado goes after Bob for child support. He is furious! He came to the house. He backed me up against the stairs. He yelled, "What the hell is the matter with you? The state of Colorado wants child support from me! I'm not paying any damn child support, so that you can run around and have a good time! If you would have behaved yourself, and had done what I told you to, we wouldn't have this problem!"

I glared at him. I pushed him. I screamed at him. "Get out of my house, and do it now, or I'll call the police!"

He yelled back at me, "You would just love it if the police would come and arrest me!"

"You damn right I would love it!" I replied.

He left, and didn't come back to the house until after Pam was born in January.

It was the last day in January, when Bob showed up. Pam was born the 23rd, and was just a week old. He looked her over from stem-to-stern, stepped to one side, and gave a slippery smile.

"Well," he said with a sly grin, "she's not mine."

I looked at him. "That's okay," I said, "I know she's mine." I had no idea that I had placed myself in a position of suspicion; I had cast a shadow of doubt. I would live with that shadow for many years.

It was a cold winter in Denver, 1962. Snow on the ground up to my knees, and five-degrees below zero. I was sick of the cold, the snow, and the slush. I promised myself that if I ever got back to Portland, Oregon, I would never complain about the rain. I wouldn't care if it rained for forty days.

It was September, 1962. Cheryl had her fourth birthday in May. Debbie had her birthday in July - she was two. Pam was eight-months-old.

Bob had been placed on probation, for non-payment of child support. He came to the house in the middle of September. He wanted us to go back together. He figured if we went back together, he wouldn't have to pay his child support. I figured it was a way back to Portland. I knew that I would not stay with Bob, after I became a resident. We used each other to get what we wanted.

We left Denver on the 3rd of October, and arrived in Portland, on the 5th, one week before the Columbus Day storm on October 12th, 1962. We were staying with Susie and Maynard, Bob's mother and stepdad.

It was late in the afternoon, when the wind began to blow, the limbs on the trees were whipping around like snowflakes in a windstorm. I was standing by the window, when a hard gust of wind blew a piece of paper against the window pane. It sounded like a bullet from a gun. The phone rang. It was Maynard telling me to stay away from the windows. The wind could blow out the glass. Just about that time, the electricity went out and the phone went dead. I was alone with the children. I found a flashlight in the desk drawer, found some matches and candles. Cheryl and Debbie were old enough to eat sandwiches. I fed Pam some baby food, and we went to bed at eight to stay warm. I have no idea what time they came home.

The following morning, we went outside to survey the damages. Trees were down, and windows had blown out of businesses and houses. We were without electricity for three days.

The first of November came, and we moved to a duplex off 86th and Powell. Bob and I were at odds with each other. He didn't have a job, he was getting unemployment compensation. I didn't know how long I could last. The tension was so thick, you could cut it with a knife.

Susie and Maynard invited us for Thanksgiving dinner. We spent the night on Wednesday. Susie was up early on Thanksgiving. She put the turkey in the oven, got herself dressed, and Bob took her to the tavern. Susie had left me a note asking me to fix the salad, peel the potatoes, make a relish tray, and they would be back at three in the afternoon.

I was furious!

You would think they could stay home on a holiday. I thought it would be nice to have a good dinner with your family. I guess they don't think the same way. Someday, I promised myself that things would be different for my children and me. I was going to find a man who believed family was important. I am sick of the way things are going around here. I'm sure that they won't be home at three. If they are, they will be drunk, and fighting with each other.

They came back at three - I was surprised. They were having a good time with each other for a change. We had a wonderful dinner. Maynard went to the store and brought back three pumpkin pies. We had some good fresh coffee with our pie.

Christmas came and went, as did New Years'. Time was just dragging by. I had nine months to go before I became a resident of Oregon, then I could leave Bob and go on Welfare.

It was the middle of March, 1963, when Janice came from Denver to stay with us.

A cold east wind was blowing, the kind of cold that gripped your bones. It was ten a.m. I heard the knock on the door. I opened the door and there stood a policeman. I was startled.

"What brings you out on a cold morning like today?" I asked the kind-looking officer. He handed me a note.

"There's an emergency in Denver. You need to call your mother as soon as possible." I thanked him and shut the door.

"What was that all about?" Bob wanted to know.

I gave a sharp glance. "I don't know at the moment. I need to go across the street to the phone booth, and call my mother to find out. Do you have any change? I don't know if she will accept a collect call or not." He dug around in his pants pockets, and managed to come up with a dollar's worth of change.

"This is all I have," he replied. I thanked him and put on my coat.

Janice yelled at me, "Wait a minute! I'm going with you!" Our teeth were chattering as we crossed the street. I placed the dime in the slot of the phone, and dialed 'O' for the operator. I gave her the number I wanted in Denver, and told her it was a collect call. I heard the operator ask my mother if she would accept a collect call, and heard her say yes.

I said to her, "What happened?"

She replied, "It's your dad. He was found dead yesterday in his apartment."

I cleared my throat, "Mother, just a minute. I'll let you talk to Janice - she's standing right beside me."

I heard Janice say "Yes, okay, I see." She told Mother that we would see her in a couple of days."

Bob was anxious to find out what happened. "Well, what happened?" I was nervous and scared. "It's our dad. He was found dead in his apartment yesterday. I don't have any details." I turned and glanced at Janice. "How about you? Do you know anything more about the event?"

"No," she replied. "I did tell Mother that we would see her in a couple of days. Mother was anxious to let me know it was important that we attend the funeral." She also went on to say that he was your dad, no matter what you thought of him, and we all know he was a devil in sheep's clothing"

Bob volunteered to take care of the children. I was a little concerned; it was a big job for him to take on. Cheryl was four, Debbie two, and Pam, fourteen-months-old.

We had an old fifty Chevy; Bob was generous, and loaned us the car. We packed our clothes and left the following morning at six a.m. We got as far as Pendleton, Oregon, when the car overheated. We pulled into a station at the end of town. We asked if we could leave our car for a week. We were headed to Denver for a funeral, and there is something wrong with the car, and we don't have the money to fix it.

The owner of the station wanted to know how long we were going to leave the car, and how we were going to get it later? We told him that we had friends in Denver, who would loan us a car, and would have access to a tow bar, and then we would be back. We exchanged phone numbers. We gave him our mother's number, and we had his number. He assured us he would take good care of the car, and showed us where we could leave it. We had to push the car; a couple of strong men came out of the station and helped us.

We got the car in a safe place. Janice looked at me with a questionable look, and asked, "Just how are we going to get to Denver? We have a hundred dollars between us."

"Well," I said with more assurance than I felt, "we can hitch-hike."

"Okay," said my sister, "let's do it."

We stood on Highway 30, stuck our thumbs out, and the first truck that came, stopped. He was a rough looking guy. He had black hair and dark brown eyes. His voice was low and gruff. "Where are you girls going? he asked.

"We are going to Denver," we replied.

"Well," he said in a low voice, "hop in. I'm going right through Denver."

Were we scared? Yes. Did we want to admit that to each other? No, of course not, but we kept our eyes on him at all times.

We arrived in Denver the following day. We showed him where to let us off, so we could take the bus. When we arrived at Mother's house, she wanted to know what we used for transportation. She didn't see a car. I placed my hands behind my back, stepped forward a step-or-two, looked her in the eye. "We took the bus." That part was true; we took the city bus. It was the details that I left out.

Dad's funeral was the first of April, April Fool's Day. How appropriate! The thought occurred to me that he was a fool. He lived a life of a fool. Always looking for something he couldn't have: money that was lost, love he couldn't find, character that he didn't have. Character that he didn't know how to build.

As I sat in the audience, and viewed the people who attended his service, I wondered how they viewed my dad. How did they know him? People came from a Baptist Church who never knew he had children. His lodge members knew him in a different way.

They knew him as a good story-teller, a man who was kind, smooth, and could tell good jokes. He could play the part of Santa Claus, and be as smooth as glass. Charming he was, he could charm the birds out of their nests, and sell snow to the Eskimos. What does that have to do with a man's character? Nothing, only his reputation.

What I felt that day, has never left. I felt a deep sadness, like a cold fog that grips the trees. I still feel that sadness. We knew him from the outside in; we never knew him from the inside out.

We decided against borrowing a car from Janice's friend. There was an ad in the paper, saying that we could drive a car from Denver, to Seattle. It was for a car dealership. We left the following day. We drove to Pendleton, rented a tow-bar, put it on the fifty Chevy, and towed it to Portland.

Bob and Janice drove the car for the dealership to Seattle, and took the bus back to Portland.
Bob discovered the water pump went out in the car. It was easy to fix, so he was happy one more time. Janice was looking for work in Portland, but couldn't find what she wanted. She decided to go back to Denver, which was a good decision for her. I knew I wasn't going to stay with Bob.

I felt like I was drifting from one day to the next. Life had no meaning, and I knew I was just putting in my time until I could leave him. We lived on food stamps and odd jobs that Bob was able to get. Sometimes, he painted houses with his uncle Steve. I knew he was not going to get steady employment. The months dragged by, summer came and went. We moved again, this time to a house. I was happy about the house: it had two bedrooms, a nice large kitchen, living room, and a fenced-in yard.

When Bob worked with his uncle, he always got paid Friday night. Friday night came, and Bob didn't come home from work. Suppertime came and went; the kids and I ate without him. I knew he was probably at the tavern. I had come to the end of my rope. I knew I was finished, and there was no point in talking to him about it. Whatever I would say, would fall on deaf ears. I began to plan how I was going to stay long enough, to be able to apply for Aid to Dependent Children.

The following morning, I decided I would call a friend of mine. She had several children, and knew how Bob was treating me. She asked me on several occasions, how long I planned on staying with Bob; how long was I willing to put up with his stuff? The choice was mine, no-one else could choose for me.

I called my friend, Colleen, and told her I was going to leave Bob. I asked if I would I be able to stay at her house for a few days? She very kindly said, "Of course, for as long as necessary."

Bob didn't come home, until Saturday afternoon. I didn't bother to ask where he had been. I just pretended that I was glad he was home. I decided I would wait until Monday, to move to Coleen's. Bob was pleasant. I went about the household chores as if everything was okay. I prepared a good dinner on Saturday night, cooked good meals on Sunday. Monday morning, I fixed his breakfast, packed his lunch, and kissed him goodbye. He went to work, as if everything at home was good. He had no idea his family would be gone when he returned that evening. I didn't leave a note.

It was Tuesday; I was beginning to feel nervous, scared, tense and upset. I didn't know what Bob was going to do or say, when he discovered we had gone. It was Wednesday evening, when we heard a loud knock at the door. Bob didn't wait for anyone to see who was on the porch – he entered the house like a hurricane. His face was red, his eyes were huge, his voice loud.

He screamed, "What the hell are you doing over here? What in the hell is the matter with you?"

Colleen stepped into the room, gave Bob a sharp look. She placed her hands on her hips. "You know, I don't allow folks to come in here to have temper tantrums. If you have something to say, you can quit your yelling and say it in a civil tone of voice. Or, you can leave. The choice is yours. Take it or leave it; I really don't give a damn."

He stopped and stared at her. He didn't know what to say. He took a deep breath, as if he was gathering his thoughts. His voice was soft, as he looked at me tenderly, "I would like for you to come home."

My eyes filled with tears, my hands shook, and my legs felt jittery. I could feel the tears on my face. My voice shook with emotion. "I'm not coming home. This is the end of the line. I'm to the end of my rope. I can't take anymore from you. You seem to find fault with everything that I do."

I knew at that moment he was beyond angry - he

was furious! He raised his fist. "You'll be sorry! I'll kill you before I'll let anyone else have you. You are mine, and no one else will have you! You couldn't find another man who would take care of you like I've taken care of you!"

I cleared my throat, stood up straight. "I'm going to thank God that I won't find another man who will take care of me like you didn't. I'll be moving home again when you leave. You can call me to let me know when you have moved."

He took a cigarette out of his shirt pocket, lit it, took a drag, inhaled deeply, and slowly blew out the smoke. He walked slowly from the room, opened the door, turned toward me and yelled, "Just where in the hell do you think I'm supposed to go? I don't have any money! I'm only working part-time painting houses with my uncle, and we can only paint when the weather is good!"

I wanted to laugh, but smiled instead. "You can go and stay with your mother. I'm sure she would like your company. She could always have a ride to the tavern. Both of you would be company for each other. Then you can exchange notes about how rotten I was."

He slammed the door on his way out. He called three days later, to let me know he had moved.

The children and I moved back home. When I opened the front door, I found he had trashed the house. The house plants were dumped on the floor, flower pots were broken, dirt was scattered everywhere. The clothes were taken out of the closet, and thrown on the bed. Dresser drawers were emptied onto the floor. I wanted to strangle him to death. Never did I ever dream, that he could be so cruel!

The thought never entered my mind, that he must have felt lost and betrayed, and the only way he could act would be to show his anger. Both of us were emotionally entangled, with no sense of reality. It would be years later that I would discover both of us were betrayed by our parents, and our course of action would be through anger and rage. The only tools we had, were anger and revenge.

We had no idea that revenge only takes place in the halls of your mind.

He called two weeks later and wanted to talk to me. He realized he was sorry for all the things he had done. I heard all this stuff before, and knew it would be only a matter of time before he would be back to his old self one more time. I could feel myself struggling with: 'I don't want to hear it again'. Maybe, this time he is telling the truth. Maybe, just maybe, I could listen one more time. The least I could do is listen to his story, but I don't have to believe it. Of course, I told him to come over, as the kids would like to see him. "Just remember, I'm only going to listen to what you have to say. I'm not making any promises of any kind."

He seemed to be okay - his voice was gentle and tender. "Okay," he replied, "I'll see you in a half-hour."

He knocked at the door. I opened it, and there he stood with a dozen red roses. He had never brought me flowerers before. I was impressed. Something said to me, *"Be careful. Something is wrong. Watch what you are doing. Pay attention to what he is saying. Pay close attention to what he doesn't say."*

I was stunned! I didn't know what to say. I was a jumble of nerves. I managed to say,
"I'll go and get a vase for the flowers." I filled the vase with water, and placed the roses in the vase. We went into the living room. The children were excited to see their dad. It was a nice day in February. Bob and the kids went outside to play. I went into the kitchen to make coffee. Sometimes, it's easier to sort things out over a cup of coffee.

He walked into the kitchen, stood by the table, lit a cigarette, and kindly asked, "Can we have a talk?"

I was nervous; my insides were shaky. "Yes, we can have a serious talk, under one condition."

He looked at me with a hint of sadness in his eyes. "What is it?"

I crossed my arms across my chest. "I don't want you to raise your voice under any circumstances. I want the right to disagree with you. You can get as angry as you want to, after you leave."

I could tell by the way he cleared his throat, that he wasn't too happy, but he agreed. We sat down at the kitchen table with two cups of coffee.

He placed his hands on the table, palms up, took my hands in his, and looked into my eyes. "I've been doing a lot of thinking. I know I have been mean and cruel to you. I've said things to you I didn't mean. I could have been more help to you, instead of expecting you to do everything."

I told myself to be careful - this is where he becomes charming and cunning. Remember, this is where you start believing everything he says.

I felt my body tighten up, and I felt shaky inside. I didn't want my voice to be shaky, so I took a deep breath. "It's like this: it's not only the things you have said to me. The times you go to the tavern, the remarks you make about women. For example, when you see a woman walking down the street, you make comments about how big her boobs are. You say things like, 'just look at the way she swings her hips. I wonder how good she is in bed? I wish YOU could move like that in bed.' Not only do I find it offensive, I want to slap your face. I want to scream, 'what in the hell is the matter with you?' Do you even understand what I'm talking about? I'm not here for you to make fun of, and furthermore, I'm not going to put up with any more of it. I am finished! Do you hear me? I'm finished!"

His eyes filled with tears. He stood beside his chair, looking sad and lost. He said, "I guess this is it, the end of the line. I was hoping it wouldn't end like this."

I watched as he slowly walked to the door, opened it, went to his car, and left. I felt empty inside, hollow, lifeless like a robot. I didn't cry. I went about my chores, and took care of the children as if everything was just fine.

The house was silent. The children were taking a nap. The silence was shattered by the ringing of the phone. It was Bob. His voice was shrill and sharp: "I want you to know I've filed a petition against you. You are an unfit mother and I'm taking you to court!"

I was furious. I screamed at him: "You have to prove that I'm an unfit mother! Furthermore, if I lose custody of these children because of something you've said, I will choke you to death!"

He yelled, "Are you threatening me?"

"No," I replied. "I'm promising you that I'll strangle you with my bare hands."   I hung up on him. My hands were shaking like leaves in a windstorm. Tears ran down my face. I had no idea what was going to happen. I only knew the children were all I had. They were my life. If I lost them because of him, I knew I would destroy him.

The court date came, and I had to bring the children. I was beyond scared. The children were not allowed in the courtroom.

The first thing the judge asked was, "Are you paying any child support?" Bob replied that he wasn't paying child support. The judge began to read the petition: "The mother is having an affair with an adult male. She is frequenting the tavern and leaving her children alone."

The judge wanted to know if Bob could prove any of the statements. He replied that he couldn't; it was only what he had heard.

She cleared her throat, and gave him a sharp look. "First of all, you are not paying any child support. You will be back in this courtroom in one month. We don't take children away from mothers, based on what we hear. You have to prove these allegations. I am making the children awards of the court for one year. They will be supervised by Childrens' Services, and they will stay with their mother. Court is dismissed."

He was furious when he left the courtroom. He looked at me with fire coming from his eyes. "I'm not paying child-support, do you hear me? I'm not going to supply you with any money!"

I didn't reply. I went to the room where the

children were playing with toys, and we left. He moved to Michigan a month later.

I had no idea I would be emotionally entangled with Bob for many years to come. I didn't know I would carry the emotional baggage with me to the next marriage. It would be many years later, before I would be able to work through the emotional entanglement.

Once again, I moved to Columbia Villa. This time, I was alone with three children. Cheryl was six, Debbie four, and Pam two. I was receiving benefits from Aid to Dependent Children; I had no job skills, no high school diploma.

Wayne and I stayed in touch with each other. He knew about the situation with Bob. His brother, Maynard, was married to Bob's mother, Susie. Bob and I were divorced in 1964. After the divorce, Susie informed me she would never speak to me again. I was devastated, sad, and overwhelmed with grief.

Christmas, 1964, Wayne called and asked if he could come over. He had some Christmas gifts for the girls. I told him he could. He said he would be there at eight o'clock. Eight came and went but Wayne didn't show up. I began to worry, as he was always on time. He called at nine to let me know he was on his way; he had a fight with his girlfriend. I told him that was probably the best thing that ever happened to him.

December 20th, 1965, Wayne and I were married in Reno, Nevada. Wayne was forty-four-years old, and had an instant family - a wife and three girls. I was twenty-six. Wayne was dependable, loyal, a man of few words, who spoke volumes in the way he lived.

15

For twenty-six years, I had lived a life of chaos. I had just stepped into a world that was dependable. This was a brand-new place to me, a world I know nothing about. I don't know what the rules are. I just know that the first argument Wayne and I have, he will tell me to pack my bags and hit the road. It doesn't happen, and I'm nervous and scared, wondering when it's going to happen. I discover that when we do have a disagreement, he doesn't argue about it – he simply walks away. I am furious! I'm used to people yelling, screaming, slamming doors. Whoever can get the maddest, gets their own way.

He walks away – what in the world do I do about it? I don't know what to do when it's okay to agree to disagree. He can have his opinion, and I can have mine. He also takes good care of his mother. I'm not used to that, either. Wayne was a man of integrity – he loved God, his church, his family and work. He was a heavy equipment operator for the same company, for almost fifty years.

In 1966, we purchased a house on 45th and Ogden. I knew I was rich – we had three bedrooms upstairs, a full basement with two bedrooms and half-bath, and a full bathroom upstairs. We had a large yard, with an apple tree in the backyard, room for a garden, a fishpond, a garage and a covered patio.

Wayne's mother, Emeline, was sixty-nine-years old, when Wayne and I got married. He was the oldest of five children. His father died when Wayne was eight-years old, and his mother was pregnant with her last child, Janet. Wayne took responsibility for the care of his mother.

Emeline was not happy about Wayne's marriage. I was eighteen-years younger than Wayne, and her youngest son, Maynard, was married to my first husband's mother. Emeline was a step-grandmother to my first husband. Wayne was his uncle by marriage. What was he thinking, marrying a woman so many years younger than he was, with three kids? He must have taken leave of his senses.

She was not happy. What was wrong with him? Now she's pregnant. She wasn't sure it was Wayne's baby, because in her mind, she had decided Wayne was getting too old to produce a child. Sheldon arrived February 23, 1967. I always called Emeline 'Grandma Wynn'. She picked him up, looked him over from stem-to-stern. She handed him to Wayne, and said, "Well, I guess he's a Wynn." She never mentioned it again. She decided that I was part of the family. From then on, I was okay.

Wayne was delighted with Sheldon. He rocked him in the rocking chair, fed him his bottle, changed his diapers, and hung diapers on the clothesline. He would carry clothespins in his shirt pocket, when he hung diapers on the line. I asked him one day, if he wondered what the neighbors thought about him hanging diapers. He looked at me and said, "No, I don't care."

. Life went on in a dependable routine that I wasn't used to. I didn't realize I was depressed. I wasn't happy about anything – I yelled at the kids and called them names. I had no parenting skills.

November 7th, 1968, Arthur was born. Wayne was delighted that he had two boys - now he had five children.

Wayne and Grandma Wynn took care of each other. I wasn't used to people looking out for each other. In the world that I came from, you looked out for yourself. I don't ever remember going home to tell my mother that I had a fight with someone at school. I learned to fight my own battles. My mother was not able emotionally, to give me any support. My dad was a different story. He was interested in himself. Inside the house, he was a beast, hot tempered, short fused, screamed at his children, and yelled at our mother. If you were to meet him out in public, he was polite, charming, and could charm birds out of their nests. You would not believe that he ever swore at his kids.

He said, 'we were enough to drive Jesus Christ off the cross;' 'we wouldn't amount to anything;' 'the apple doesn't roll too far from the tree;' 'women give fifty-thousand dollars-worth away, before they learned to charge for it.'

He asked me what size bra I wore, number one cup or number two? When he would tell me that the apple doesn't roll too far from the tree, I would tell him, "This apple is going so far, you will not know what tree it came from". I promised myself as a young girl, that I wouldn't live my life the same way my mother and dad lived theirs.

I learned to argue with my dad - I called him 'Old Man'. I learned to blackmail him. He had a girlfriend, who mother knew nothing about. I used to say to my dad, "If you don't want mother to know where you were last night, you'll give me the money to go roller-skating," or where ever it was that I wanted to go.

I had many bad habits. I learned to smoke cigarettes when I was ten-years-old. My dad taught me how to roll my own. I was a steady smoker by the time I was twelve. I knew all the cuss words. I could be a bully inside of the house, and very charming out in public. I made friends with all types of people. I knew people who were tough, and folks who went to church on a regular basis.

My world has been turned upside down. I know about people who are kind and loving to each other, but I don't know the rules. I know how to stuff things inside me, but I don't know how to share the inside of me. I don't know how I feel.

Wayne does not smoke; he doesn't like cigarettes. I smoke two-packs-a-day. I smoke everywhere. My cigarettes are my friends. Wayne is concerned about my smoking. He does the only thing he knows to do: he brings articles to me about cigarette smoking, and how bad it is for you. He tells me he doesn't want me to die from smoking. Do I think he has my best interest at heart? Of course not. I begin to smolder.

"Well," I say to myself, "what's the matter with him? He knew I smoked when I married him. If he thinks I'm going to quit just because he doesn't like it, well, he had better think again."

Of course, I don't tell him what I'm thinking. I

just keep on smoking. I buy my cigarettes by the carton. If I only have three packages of cigarettes left, I know I need to buy another carton. I have no clue how bad everything smells. The house, my clothes, or the car. My fingers are brown - even my skin has a yellow tinge, and my breath stinks. The dirty ashtrays that are in every room, give a moldy aroma to every corner of the house. I know I need to quit smoking, but I don't know how to quit. What do people do with their hands, when they don't smoke?

It was February,1971, and my neighbor's husband had a heart attack. I have just come home from the doctor's office. My physician informed me that if I didn't quit my smoking, I could die from lung cancer. I explained to him that I would rather die of lung cancer, than emphysema. His response was, "What makes you think you have a choice?"

Later that evening, I took my neighbor's wife to the hospital, to see her husband. I overheard two nurses talking to each other. One of them said to the other, "I wish we could do for cancer patients, what we can do for heart patients."

That conversation hit me like a bolt of lightning. I felt the tension in myself as I took a deep breath. Something told me I was meant to hear that conversation.

The following morning, I saw an ad in the newspaper. Portland Adventist Hospital was giving a five-day quit-smoking class. The price was right - it was free. I called to see when it was taking place, and told them to sign me up. Three days later, at seven in the evening, I attended my first quit-smoking class. I learned that evening, that when you smoke, your lungs turn black. They showed us pictures of what your lungs look like when you smoke. It takes five-to-seven years for your lungs to turn pink.

I had work to do; this was not going to be an easy task, to quit smoking. I had to teach myself to quit. The first step, was when I left that evening, I had to throw my cigarettes away in the trashcan at the door. I cried when I threw them away. I threw my ashtrays away when I got home. I knew that if I found anything to smoke, including a cigar, I would be smoking it. I was not to have anything that contained caffeine, such as coffee, tea, hot chocolate, soda pop, etc. What in the world was I going to drink at breakfast? What do people drink when they don't drink coffee? I went to the grocery store and bought something that looked like coffee, but turned out to be a kind of cereal drink. It was awful. I drank water, lots of water. I discovered that water really did taste pretty good. After dinner, I went for a walk instead of sitting at the dinner table, smoking. It only takes three days to get nicotine out of your body. It takes at least six months, or longer, to get the habit out of your head.

    Wayne was so proud of me when I quit smoking, that he went out and bought me a dozen roses and card. It said, 'Congratulations on your success for not smoking'. I knew I could never smoke
again, and disappoint Wayne. I also knew that he loved me dearly. I was the love of his life. I told Wayne later, that if I ever started smoking again, I would smoke until I died. I would never go through this agony again.

    I learned what people did with their hands, when they didn't smoke. They washed dishes without an ashtray on the drainboard, ironed clothes, cooked, cleaned the house, and all the other chores they have always done, without an ashtray. A year later, I was at a friend's house. Her husband had left a package of cigarettes on the table. I decided I would see what one of those cigarettes would taste like. I took one out of the package, lit it up, took a big drag, and inhaled the smoke down my throat. My eyes watered, I coughed after I let the smoke out of my mouth, and I decided that those cigarettes would kill a human. I never tried it again.

16

It was 1974, and I decided it was time for me to get a high school diploma. I attended night classes. I was thirty-five when I received my GED.

It would seem from all outside appearances, that my life would be getting better instead of worse. Our family was attending church. The children appeared to be happy, but their mother was an emotional wreck. I was depressed. I wanted to break every window in the house, starting with the windows in the kitchen. I wanted to scoop everything off the counters and throw it on the floor. I wanted to scream, and pull my hair out. The children could do nothing right. If they went out to pick vegetables that grew in the garden, the berries, or the walnuts, I would never tell them what a good job they did. I criticized them for what they missed. Life began to take its toll.

My oldest daughter left home; the second one had run away from home; the third one was chronically running away. Was I going to hold myself responsible for any of the decisions my kids were making? Of course not. If you had kids who acted like mine, you would act like me. Pam was putting me through an emotional wringer. She was placed in foster care, and was assigned a case worker. Her name was Pat. Pat talked to Wayne and me about our backgrounds, and what kind of family systems we had come from.

Wayne's family system was supportive, my family system was dysfunctional. I had a mentally ill mother, my dad was abusive. I didn't trust women - they were either sick or crazy, men were either next to God, or they were bastards. I was lonely, depressed, sad, and angry. I couldn't share myself with Wayne. I didn't know how. When there was any kind of problem, I knew I had to fix it. I had no clue how my behavior affected Wayne, or how he must have felt when I would not, could not, share myself with him.

I knew my life was in shambles; I didn't know I

was the problem. I believed I was smart enough to figure it out. I was smart, but the problem was, I had no clue about emotions, feelings, or human behavior. The only feeling I really knew about, was anger. I knew in the household where I came from, in order to get your own way, we learned that whoever could slam the door the hardest, scream, cuss, or have the biggest temper tantrum, could get their own way. Of course, what worked for me as a child, didn't work in the adult world. I was now in a world where people talked about what was going on, but had a solution to the problem. I had no tools to work with; I was lost. I had to make a new path, a different way of living. I felt like I was in a forest, overgrown with weeds. I was cutting a new path with a machete.

Wayne and I met with the caseworker. She was a smart, insightful woman. She was stern but kind, when she told us that I needed to be in therapy. She told Wayne I was a smart woman, but too many bad things had happened to me. I had too many missing pieces that needed to be put together. "She can't do it alone, she needs guidance, tools to work with. She needs to go to therapy today - tomorrow may be too late." When we went home that day, I called and made an appointment with a therapist.

God always knows what we really need. He knew I needed a male therapist. My first session and I thought, "What does he know? He's a man." The first thing I told him, was that if he had the kids I had, he would act like me. I think he belonged to the uh-huh club, as that was his only response. I went every week. Every week I went, he would ask "How do you feel, Sandra?" My response was always the same, "I don't know."

Finally, when he asked me that same question, I told him if I knew how I felt; I wouldn't be there. "Good," he said, "that's the answer I was looking for."

I began to make some progress, but it was hard work. The first thing I had to face, was the fact that I was responsible for my actions, my behavior, and my feelings. When I heard that, I was furious!

"What do you mean, I'm responsible for my behavior? My mother was crazy, and my daddy was mean."

The therapist replied, "What does that have to do with the present time? Did you have the power to fix any of the problems your mother or father had? If you could have fixed it, would you have liked the results?"

That was a question I had never asked myself. I still wonder what the answer would have been. I have come to realize, that none of us get to choose our parents. If we could choose, would we make the right choice? Those are questions that have no easy or simple answers.

The therapist finally became human, in my thinking. In the world that I came from, men had no feelings; they couldn't be trusted. The only touch they knew, would be sexual. To know something with your head, and to feel it with your feelings, are worlds apart. I started to give myself permission to feel his tenderness, his caring for me as another human being. He slipped his arm around my shoulder for the first time, and I felt safe and secure. To be able to accept his touch at a feeling where we were level, was a giant step for me. The tears flowed freely down my cheeks. He quietly spoke the words, "Give yourself permission to know, and to believe, that you are likeable and loveable." I couldn't talk - I was too choked up with emotion. That was the beginning of a turning point. There was no turning back. It was a new path for me.

I began to realize, I was living a life of quiet discontent. I was a shadow unto myself. I stood and looked at my family, my friends, the church and life itself, from the outside in. I would not allow myself to be a part of anything. Even God was viewed from the outside-in. I was an outsider looking in the windows. I could see them, but they couldn't see me.

It was a warm summer evening. Dinner was over, the dishes washed and put away. I went out to the garden to pick the beans. Grandma Wynn was hoeing around the carrots, and Wayne was watering the plants. As I was picking the beans, I began to sob deep sobs, sobs that came from the bottom of my feet. Wayne came over to me, wrapped his arms around me, held me like a child. In a soft voice, he said, "What in the world is wrong?"

It took a few seconds before I could talk. "I finally belong here."

He tipped my chin back, wiped the tears from my eyes. He gently said, "I could have told you that you belong here."

I looked up at him. "You don't get it. I belong here emotionally."

"I don't understand," he replied.

"It's okay. I get it, and you don't have to get it." My world seemed to be a little brighter. I began to feel comfortable with who I was. I was beginning to feel calm inside. My world was beginning to feel right side up.

Pam is in a foster home. Does she stay there? No. She is placed in another foster home, and she runs again. By this time, the case worker decides Pam is not going to stay in any foster home. The plan was to place her in the Christie Home. The home would not accept you if you were pregnant. Pam had decided she was not going to the home, because it was a locked-down facility. She disappeared to California. The State Police brought her back to Oregon. Pam was happy. She was pregnant, and could not go to the Christie Home. She was placed at the White Shield Home for Girls. She could go to school, obtain her high school diploma, and give birth to her baby.

I was relived. I knew where Pam was, and she couldn't run away. I also felt emotionally entangled - she was going to have a baby who she could not take care of. I felt like I was living a drama that I couldn't see the end of. The home provided counseling for Pam, and was good for her. I was aware that she heard what they said, but the problem was, she did not apply it to herself.

Pam was doing a good job at White Shield. She was going to school, earning good grades, and taking good care of herself. Pam was smart - she learned quickly, and was charming. She knew how to manipulate the system. She was good at telling me what I wanted to hear. I believed Pam would do the right thing. I was emotionally wound up, my stomach was in knots, my hands were sweaty and my heart was pounding.

It was a cold, rainy, and gray day. The wind was blowing, the trees were waving their branches, and the leaves were flapping. I sat across from Pam, when she folded her arms, looked at me with her soft green eyes, and quietly asked me, "What should I do with the baby?"

My eyes filled with tears. I felt a lump in my throat, and my voice was soft when I answered, "I don't know, Pam. The decision isn't mine to make. I do have a suggestion, if you would like to hear."

"Yes," she replied "I would like to hear it. "

I cleared my throat, and took a deep breath. "Pam, if I were you, I would take a sheet of paper and draw a line down the middle. On one side of the page, I would write the benefits of keeping the baby, and what you could give the child. On the other side of the line, I would write the benefits of putting the baby up for adoption. It will not be an easy decision; you will have to decide what is best for you and the child. Whatever you decide, I will stand beside you. You don't have much time left, as your baby is due in six weeks." We wrapped our arms around each other and wept.

As I left and walked to the car, I felt the weight of the world on my shoulders. I couldn't tell her what to do, and I couldn't fix things for her. At that moment, I thought it was easier to be angry at the situation, than to feel the hurt and the pain. There is a price to pay for anger. It is healthier to feel your pain. It seemed like I was floating from one day to the next. I was numb. I went about my chores like a robot. It seemed to be too hard to think or to feel.

I was in the basement, folding the laundry, when the phone rang and broke the silence that had gripped the room. I was startled, and my voice was shaky when I answered the call, "Is Sandra Wynn available?"

"Yes, she is," I replied. "What can I help you with?"

"My name is Mary. I work at the White Shield Home, and I'm calling to let you know that Pam has had her baby. You can go to see her at OHSU."

I thanked her for the information. As I drove to the hospital, I felt heavy inside, as if I was carrying a block of cement in my stomach. Pam had decided a few weeks earlier, to give the baby up for adoption. I felt peaceful with her decision. I also felt tearful and sad, that Pam had placed herself in the position she was in.

I made up my mind, that I was not going to make this any more difficult than it already was. I had my speech prepared. It was time for me to hold this new little baby who has come into the world, to feel his warm little body, look at his fingers and toes. I ran my fingers across his soft little face, and looked into his soft blue eyes. I sat and rocked him, and told him how much I loved him. I tried to explain to him how special he was, and there was a special Mom and Dad coming to take him home. I wanted him to know that his birth-mother was not able to take care of him. She was giving him the
best gift she could, by sharing her baby with a special Mom and Dad. My eyes filled with tears as I told him I was his Grandma, and I would never forget him. He would live forever in my heart. I don't know how long the nurse had been standing there, waiting to take the baby to his new parents. I placed the baby in her arms. I told him goodbye, and that I loved him.

I went in to see Pam, before I left to go home. I sat on her bed, wrapped my arms around her, and we wept together. As I left to go home, I was hopeful that Pam had learned something from this experience. I knew deep inside of me, that it was a lesson she would never forget. I knew that I had many unanswered questions I would ponder, for the rest of my life. Was I responsible for the decision Pam made? Did I, in some way, force her to make the choices she made? Could I have done things differently? I didn't know, and I will probably never know the answer to those questions. It seems those are complicated questions, with no simple answers. I felt heavy inside, weighted down, a foreboding dread of coming events. My thoughts were consumed with Pam. The stage was set. This was the beginning of events that would turn me inside out.

Pam was beginning a new chapter in her life. She had graduated from high school with high honors. She found a job at Holgate Center, and rented a one-bedroom apartment. I told her how proud I was of her, and told her she was smart. She was clean and sober; she couldn't do enough for me. There was a nagging voice that I didn't want to listen to. Be careful, the picture she is painting may not be as wonderful as she is making it appear. I didn't pay attention. Things began to fall apart.

Pam knew I loved older folks, and began to talk to me about getting a job where she worked. "Mother," she said, "you would love it here. You can come to work here as a support-worker." I wanted to know what a support worker did. I didn't know anything about a care center. She went on to tell me that a support worker filled the pitchers with water that was on the night stand beside the patient's bed, and feed patients who could not feed themselves.

I was hired at the Holgate Care Center. I loved the job. I fell in love with the old folks; they spoke to my soul. It wasn't a job to me, as much as a work of my soul. I knew I wanted to do more for the patients. The time came when they offered to train me as a CNA. I took the course, and loved the position of service it provided for me. For the first time in my life, I felt I was being of service to humanity.

Pam began to fall back into her old way of life. She started calling in on a regular basis. She was sick, and couldn't make it to work. As a result of her lack of attendance, she lost her job. I saw less and less of her, and knew deep inside that things were not right, things I wasn't talking about. I couldn't talk about them, they were too painful.

She couldn't pay her rent. She received an eviction notice, and had thirty days to move. She asked if she could move back home. I told her Wayne and I would talk it over. This was new behavior for me. In the past, I would have handled it myself, and tell him later what I did, never stopping to think about how he would feel about it. When Wayne came home from work, and dinner was over, we sat down to decide what we were going to do.

The first thing we did was lay out the facts. Pam had been out of the house for a long time. Did we want her back in, with all the chaos she would bring with her? The answer was no. So, how could we keep her out in a pleasant way, and be firm with our decision? Pam would not abide by any rules, so we decided to make the rules so strict, that she would not abide by them anyway.

The first rule was, that she had to be home by ten o'clock, and if she stayed out all night, she would find her clothes on the front porch. That was the only rule we made, and we knew she wouldn't obey that one.

Pam called the following morning to find out what we decided. When I told her, she seemed to be okay with the decision Wayne and I made. She brought her belongings that afternoon. She left shortly, and didn't come home all night. She called the following morning, and I told her that her stuff was on the front porch. She told me she was taking care of a child, and wanted to know if she could come by with the child to get her stuff? I told her yes, as long as the child was old enough to walk, because I was not going to take her to her destination. She came to the house and picked up her items.

We were relived and sad, that Pam had not learned from her experience. We didn't know at the time what a slippery path she would take. She was on the crooked road of drugs, deception, and lies. Pam would tell me that her friends didn't use any drugs, and they were always keeping her straight. Her friends always had a problem they needed help with, and of course, Pam could help them out. Pam couldn't fix her problems, but she could always fix the other person's. She was living from place to place - I call it sleeping from couch to couch. Working here and there most of the time, and I didn't know where she was. It was probably a blessing in disguise.

Wayne was always there with a helping hand. We struggled together. He was quiet about how he felt. I could tell he simply didn't know what to do. We were two broken parents who couldn't fix the problem. Pam was no longer a small child you could pick up and put in timeout. I felt like I was walking on the razor's edge of sanity. At any moment, I could fall over the rim.

God always creates a new path - we needed some breathing room. Grandma Wynn was at the place where it was becoming difficult for her to live alone. Grandma didn't want to live with any of her children. We finally had a discussion with her, and let her know it was time for her to sell her house, and move in with us. She finally conceded. We fixed our home so she would have a kitchen, living room, and bedroom. The only thing she shared with us, was the bathroom.

We had a new project; Grandma needed us and we needed her. We kept Pam in our prayers and went on with life, as best we could.

Grandma Wynn didn't like housework, and I didn't like yard work. We made a deal: if she wouldn't do my housework, I wouldn't do her yard work. I told Grandma the yard was hers, and she could do anything she wanted to with it. She had Wayne till a space for her in the backyard, so she could plant raspberry bushes. She was happy. She received a small Social Security check every month, so we decided we would not charge her any rent. We were in charge of cooking meals. Grandma had cooked enough meals, and it was time for her to do what she wanted. She spoiled me rotten. She mended all our clothes, cooked ham and beans, made bread, doughnuts, and the best apple pie. I did Grandma's laundry (our washer and dryer were in the basement).

We took Grandma Wynn everywhere with us - if we went on vacation, she went along. We took her out to dinner, grocery shopping, to the bank, and to Reno, to visit her daughter Janet. I finally had a Mother. I didn't know how to act with a Mother who would look after me.

17

It was a warm summer day in July. I had just come into the house to answer the phone: It was a long-distance call from Denver, Colorado, from my mother's sister-in-law, Lena. Her first words were, "Your mother is in the hospital; she has lung cancer."

I felt the anger that welled up inside of me, as I yelled, "She finally has got something that will do her in!" Those words hung like stones in the air, words that should never have been spoken. I was angry and sad at the same time. I had heard all my life that she was going to kill herself, and now it was going to happen. I felt guilty for the way I felt. I apologized to Lena. I knew I shouldn't have said what I did. Mother was in a nursing home, and I knew Harry, my stepdad, would need my help.

Wayne and Grandma Wynn took care of the kids, and I went to Denver. I stayed for two weeks, and painted the kitchen. I knew Harry would have to sell the house. I went to the nursing home to take Mother to the hospital for some blood work. I went with her in the ambulance. She sat in a wheelchair, and didn't know who I was.

I have never felt as sad and lonely as I did that day. The tears rolled down my cheeks. I walked as if my legs had been painted on. She was always a thin, small woman. She was even smaller now. Her arms were crossed in her lap - they were thin, frail, and chalky-white. Her small legs hung like toothpicks. As I pushed her in the wheelchair, I wondered if she ever really lived, or was she just passing through? The lights were on, but nobody was home. As I approached the lab, I wondered if they would be able to find her vein in her tiny arm, which looked like it belonged to a six-year-old child. I knew at that moment, I loved her, and I also knew that I had never known her.

As I stood there, swirling thoughts were going through my mind, about what kind of Mother I wished I had had, and the kind of Mother I had. What I wanted, and what I received, never matched. I wanted a Mother who would bake cookies, cakes, and pies. I wanted one whom I could sit on her lap, and she would hold me and tell me how much she loved me. She would rock me in her rocking chair, and tell me how special I was. That didn't happen. My mother saw things that weren't there, heard voices that no one else heard, and lived in a scary world that I will never know.

The lab person was kind and gentle; he must have known I was an emotional wreck. As I glanced in the mirror beside me, I could see my red-swollen eyes. He quietly and gently said in a soft voice, "I'll be careful." And he was.

As I escorted mother back to the nursing home, I wondered how different my life might have been, if I would have had a different Mother and Dad. Would I be a different kind of person than I am today? Maybe that's another difficult question I will never have the answer to. I will never be able to put the missing pieces together. Mother had no coping skills for being poor. She came from a wealthy family, who were prominent and well-known. When the wealth was gone, she was lost. I think she became a lost person when her daddy died, when she was twelve.

My mother and dad lived a life of make-believe; they were the great pretenders. Their lives were filled with drama and deception. Dad was cunning and slippery - he could sell snow to the Eskimos. Mother was going to kill herself, and dad would bury her when he got home. The apartment was filled with tension. I always felt I was going to find something terrible, when I would return home. I was walking on eggshells, until I would open the door to the apartment, and find everyone inside were still alive and breathing.

There were many different scenes of drama. Sometimes, Mother would be sick in bed, or she would be pacing the floor, wringing her hands, and cussing the neighbors, because she saw two people at the end of the hall talking to each other. She just knew they were talking about her. There was no way I could convince her they weren't talking about her. If I tried to tell her they were talking about something that didn't concern her, she just knew I was on their side. Whatever that meant, I have no idea. I learned very early on, just to nod my head and go on. Maybe that was the first lesson of my learning - to block things out.

Our dad had lots of temper tantrums. He cursed his children, and told us we would never amount to anything - the apple doesn't roll very far from the tree. I had an answer for him. I would tell him that this apple was going to roll so far from the tree, that he wouldn't know what tree it came from. The drama would continue. He would sit at the end of the table, his face would be red, and he would be yelling, his eyes bulging. I would sit next to him, and stare at him. Pretty soon he would be yelling: "What the hell are you staring at?"

I would give him a blank look. "I don't know. I'm trying to figure it out."

It was sad. I learned how to get money from him, by black-mailing him. I knew he had a girlfriend. I used to tell him that if he didn't want me to tell Mother where he was the night before, he had better come up with the money I wanted.

I was his favorite; he taught me how to use men for what I wanted. I learned from my dad that men were not to be trusted; the only touch they knew about was sexual. I never sat on my dad's lap, never wrapped my arms around him, and he never ever told me he loved me. I never had a conversation with my dad. The arguments I had with my dad, gave me a false sense of power. I learned I could get my own way, if I could yell louder than he did, slam the door the hardest, or shed the most tears. It would take years for me to learn, that I was using a negative behavior pattern to get what suited me.

Life is different for me now. I have a wonderful husband, five children, a mother-in law who loves me. I will spend the rest of my life untangling the emotions that almost strangled me to death, when I was a child.

I pushed the wheelchair mother was sitting in, to her room at the nursing facility. I thanked the nurses for taking care of her. I had a lump in my throat, tears rolled down my face. The nurse put her arms around my shoulders, and I wept like a child. Was I weeping for the Mother who was dying, or for the Mother whom I never knew? I wouldn't know the answer to that question, until many years later.

As I walked the ten blocks to Mother's house, I had many swirling thoughts, like leaves being tossed by the wind. I thought of her as a young woman, and how she must have believed when she married my dad, that he would take care of her. He would love her forever, instead he turned her inside out. She was broken-hearted when they were divorced.

That was then, and this is now. It was time for me to get ready to go home to Portland. I was missing my family. I lived a different life - I was with people who were supportive and kind. A life that was predictable. I knew I would return in a few months to attend my mother's funeral.

Harry came into the room as I was packing my suitcase. He crossed his arms across his chest.
"Looks like you're getting ready to go home. I'm going to miss you, Sander.'

"I know, Harry, but I have to go home and take care of my family. You can call me, and remember, you can go to the nursing home every day to see Mother, and stay as long as you want." It was hard for me to leave him. I knew he just didn't know what to do. He adored my mother, and in his mind, he was thinking it was his job to take care of her.

I went home the following day. My thoughts and emotions were still in Denver. I was aware that I was angry, and sad at the same time. I was angry she was going to die, and sad that I never knew her.

I was a zombie, taking care of my family. Every time the phone would ring, I just knew it would be news Mother had passed away. I could feel the hole I had in my soul, of never knowing my mother emotionally. It would be years later, when I would learn how to nurture my rebellious child, and to be a good Mother to myself.

The dreaded phone call arrived, with the news that Mother had died.

My sister, Janice, and I went to Denver. The house Mother and Harry lived in was sold in three days. Harry's sister came from Illinois, to get her brother. She wanted him to live with her. She didn't want Harry to be alone My emotions were scattered. The house was gone, both parents had died, and I felt like they never lived. It seemed like a fairy tale, except nobody lived happily ever after.

I have asked myself this question many times: What drew them together? Was it the money my mother's family had? Was it his good looks? His smooth personality? The way he had with words, the promises he made to my mother? The truth is, I will never know. There are no simple answers to complicated questions.

When the funeral service was over, my sister, Janice, and I said goodbyes to our aunts and cousins. We went back to the homestead to say goodbye to Harry. He was packing his belongings to move to Illinois, to be with his sister. He looked sad, lonely, and tired.

` I stepped over to him, took his hands into mine, "Harry, I want you to know how much Janice, Karen, and I appreciate the way you took care of our mother. Thank you for making her last days on earth happy ones. Thank you for loving her. You will live in our hearts forever." Our eyes filled with tears as we said our goodbyes.

I was glad to be home once again. There was a cloud of sadness that surrounded me. Feelings of loneliness,; not being connected emotionally to my family, misunderstood, and feeling like nobody cared. I couldn't share how I felt; I had no tools to put the words into sentences that would make sense.

I relived the events that had taken place in my life as a child. I thought about how embarrassed I felt, when, as a small child, our dad would come into the kitchen, walk over to the sink, move the dishes to one side, and pee beside the dirty dishes. He would turn the water on, and wash the urine down the drain. The way we sat like zombies, never looking up, or at each other, just keeping on eating our oatmeal. The smell of urine mingling with the aroma of oatmeal and coffee, was over-whelming.

The many times our mother was going to kill herself, and run out of the apartment, down the hall, and out the back door. We would run after her, screaming and crying! She would be yelling, "I'm going to strangle myself to death!" She would put her hands around her neck, her face would turn red, and she would make a gurgling noise in her throat.

I would run after her with my two sisters behind me. We would be crying and screaming: "Mama! Mama! Don't do that! "We love you!"

Her eyes would take on a strange glare, as if she didn't know what she was doing or saying. All at once, she would stop and look at us with a strange expression, as if she had no idea what had just taken place. I always felt crazy after one of her episodes; there was no one to talk to about what just happened. Who would believe a child? I had no words to explain our lives. The sadness, loneliness, and secrets were locked inside. We were left to our own devices.

The world I left in Denver, was chaotic and crazy. The new world I lived in, was still new to me. I couldn't explain to Wayne, or to Grandma Wynn, where I had come from, or what it was like. It was unexplainable.

Pam was back to her old way of life. Down the road of drinks and drugs - the slippery road of deception. I was on the road of trying to fix her, but I had no tools in my toolbox. I just knew, that if she would listen to me, she would be okay. The many times I sobbed and begged God to fix Pam. I told God I would give my life for her. God always knows what he is doing. I just didn't know it at the time.

It was 1983, and Pam married a man from the Middle East. I decided Pam was going to settle down and create a new life for herself. That was not in her thinking. It was party time for her. It seemed to me that party time wasn't a good time. She was always in a fight with someone, or lost her money, or hadn't been home for three days.

Life is full of change. Pam was going to have a baby. She settled down during her pregnancy, stayed at home, cleaned the house, and prepared meals. I just knew this would be the time that life would change for her. August 1st, 1985, Pam gave birth to Sarah. She was so proud and happy with her new baby girl. The day I went to the hospital to take her home, I had grandson, Brandon, with me; he was five-years-old. Pam let Brandon carry Sarah in the back seat of the car on a pillow, as we went home.

Pam decided it was time for her to go to some AA meetings. She knew she needed some help, and she couldn't do it alone. I was hopeful that this was the time she would get acquainted with herself on the inside. I wanted her to know she was not alone in her addiction, that there were a lot of folks who were hiding from life.

I sat with Pam, and held Sarah in my arms. I wept when I heard folks tell about their addictions, and what they had done to their lives. I wondered if Pam would apply any of the information to her own life. Maybe it just applied to everybody else. Lots of times, information doesn't apply to us, because we are different - it's everybody else who has a problem.

I went with Pam, week after week, to AA meetings. She seemed to be taking in the information she heard. From all outside appearances, she seemed to be doing a good job of staying clean and sober.

Things began to change for Grandma Wynn; her health began to deteriorate. A few years before she came to live with us, she had one of her breasts removed, due to cancer. Grandma is eighty-nine. She is anemic and has to go in every once-in-awhile for blood transfusions. I am aware that this is the last part of her life. She is not going to be with us for long. One of the last times I took Grandma to the hospital for a blood transfusion, I felt like a little girl who was losing the only Mother I ever had. I was terrified, sad, and weeping. I pushed the wheelchair

Grandma was sitting in, into the hospital and up to the nurses' station. The nurse came and took her to her room. I stepped over to talk to the head nurse.

I placed my hands on my hips. "She is hard of hearing, incontinent, wears Depends," and then stopped myself. "Oh, my goodness! I'm sure you have had patients like her before. Just remember one thing – she's my mother-in-law, and I love her dearly." I began to weep like a child. The nurse placed her arm around my shoulder, and assured me they would take good care of her. I stepped into Grandma's hospital room to say goodbye. She looked up at me. She placed her hand on my arm. "Sandra, I'll be okay." I took Grandma home the following day.

Grandma loved Pam, and as far as she was concerned, Pam could do no wrong. It was becoming difficult for Grandma to take a shower by herself. She decided she would let Pam assist her with her showers.

I knew something was really wrong with Grandma. She was pale, her energy level was low, and she just wasn't herself. I took her to her primary care doctor. He decided she needed to go in to have a colonoscopy. She had a tumor in her colon, and was scheduled for surgery. I was worried -Grandma was ninety-years-old. Would she survive the surgery?

She made it through the surgery. She came home with a colostomy bag, and had no idea how to take care of it. I assured her I would take care of it for her.

Pam was pregnant again. I had mixed feelings. Pam didn't want to be married, she wanted her freedom. She decided that after the baby was born, she would pursue her freedom. I was hopeful one more time, that maybe she would change her mind about getting a divorce.

She continued through the pregnancy with no problems, gave birth to another beautiful baby girl. I took care of Sarah, while Pam was in the hospital with Mariam. I always called Mariam 'Mary'; she was Mary as far as I was concerned. She was Mariam as far as her father was concerned.

It seemed to me, maybe it was the beginning of the war between their dad and me. He wanted me to call her Mariam, and I called her Mary. Maybe, just maybe, I was the stubborn one. It was easier to say it was him - after all, he was from the Middle East.

Dad was taking care of the children, and Pam was out running around. Sometimes, she wouldn't come home for a couple of days. Dad took better care of the children than she did. He always made sure they were clean, and had good food to eat.

Grandma Wynn was living her last days, and she wanted to have a yard sale before she died. Her son, Richard, brought his trailer from San Francisco, to Portland. Richard and his mother sorted through her household items. I admired Richard's patience. He sat, day after day with his mother, sorting through her items. "Do you want to keep this, or that?" he would ask.

Grandma was a saver. She brought all her belongings with her from Minnesota. In her mind, if she threw anything away, she might need it someday. Someone might come by who would need the item, and she could give it to them. Sometimes I would say to her, "Well, no one has been by in fifty years - maybe you can get rid of it."

She would give me a stern look. The summer of 1986, Grandma had her yard sale. She seemed delighted that she finally got to live out one of her plans and dreams.

Grandma Wynn knew death was waiting for her. She was talking to her son, Richard, and telling him she wanted to be buried in her black dress. Richard always had a wonderful sense of humor. He said to his mother, "You don't want to be buried in that black dress! People will think you're dead! Why don't you pick the red one?"

"Okay," she said, "the red dress it is."

Richard knew his mother was getting weaker, and that Grandma was independent. She didn't want any nurse coming to help her with a shower. She decided she would allow Pam to help her with her showers. She adored Pam, and in her eyes, Pam could do no wrong.

Grandma had to go back to the doctor. She was growing weaker, and had another tumor in her colon. There was no treatment left for her. We took her home. She knew she didn't have much time left on this earth. She was not the kind of person to fuss about what was about to take place. She had her burial plot bought and paid for, along with her headstone. She had purchased a casket a few years before this event. She was in charge to the very end.

We wanted her to go to the hospital, but she refused. She would not go in an ambulance. She finally decided she would go, if she could ride in the back of Richard's truck. They made a gurney for her out of a piece of plywood, and wrapped a sheet around a piece of foam rubber. They put a blanket over her body, as she laid on the homemade gurney. She said, "Goodbye. I won't be coming back here alive."

I couldn't talk and I couldn't move - I sat like a mummy. I felt like I was watching a movie, and maybe it would soon be over; life would be normal again.

I will never forget the date. February 23rd, 1987. She was put on morphine. Brandon was eight-years-old. That was his grandma, and he wanted to go to see her. I told him she wouldn't know him. He looked at me and placed his hands on his hips. He replied, "I will know her."

She was transported to a nursing facility, three days later. We were zombies, sleep-walking through the days. Janet, Wayne's sister, and I, went to the nursing facility to make sure they were taking good care of her. We would check to see if the sheets were dry; we didn't want the sheets to be wrinkled. We made sure she was clean at all times, including her fingernails. We knew she was not going to get any better. At some emotional level, we felt better knowing they were taking good care of her.

Grandma was waiting for her last child to come home, so she could tell him goodbye. When Harry arrived at the nursing home, went to her room, and stood beside her bed, he took her hand in his, and quietly said, "I'm here, Mother." She opened her eyes and looked at him. She said in a soft voice, "Goodbye, Harry." She closed her eyes, took her last breath, and was gone.

We knew she was going to die, and thought we were prepared for it. We were at an intellectual level. Emotionally, we were in pieces. I lost the best Mother I ever had. I had a gaping hole in my soul. I couldn't talk. I felt a numbness I had never experienced before, a numbness that would be repeated a few more times in the future.

We arranged her funeral; we went through the routine of greeting folks at her service. We huddled together in a vacuum, with feelings we couldn't express. They were too deep, and too fresh. We had lost the main spoke-person in our family system. Grandma was gone - our lives began to take on a different dimension. We felt disconnected and alone. The house felt empty and cold, and there were times we didn't know what to do with ourselves. It seemed like we had more problems than we had time to solve.

I felt trapped. I had no way out, and nowhere to go. I had two precious grandbabies, Sarah and Mary, who needed a mother. Their mother was stuck in the drug world. I became their port in a storm. I had no idea at the time, how long the storm was going to last. Wayne stood beside me, supported me, and encouraged me, with his love and tenderness.

We started to realize it was time to get rid of the house. Wayne was going to retire, our funds were running out, the house needed too many repairs, and we didn't have any money. We had taken out a second mortgage to fix an apartment for Grandma, when she was with us. We wrestled with the problem, and decided to seek professional advice. We filed bankruptcy, put the house in foreclosure, and moved to a duplex on 33rd and Brooklyn.

I could feel that Wayne was devastated - to his way of thinking and doing things, you didn't file for bankruptcy - only deadbeats did. It was his job and his duty to take care of his wife and family, and he had failed. He didn't have the tools or words that I have, and I knew he carried deep feelings inside of him. We would go for a walk, hold hands, and I would softly say to him, "Wayne, it is okay where we are. I like it here." He would squeeze my hand in his.

He accepted things the way they were. He finally realized, there are times when a chain of events happen that you can't change, and you don't have to like the choice you had to make. You learn how to live with it. I was having a difficult time getting along with my grandchildrens' dad. He was strict, rigid, and hot tempered; he was the only one that knew anything. He was doing things according to his culture, and I was in my culture. His Middle Eastern ways didn't match my way of thinking. It was difficult for him- he was working, going to school, and taking care of two young children. He needed some assistance with the girls, and we were always available to give him a helping hand.

Sarah was twenty-two months old, and Mary eight-months old, when Pam lost custody of them. Children Services of Oregon, had been involved with Pam and their dad, for several months. Pam was not to leave the State of Oregon. It was not a part of her behavior to pay attention to rules or regulations; she always did what she wanted to.

18

It was a warm Monday morning in June,1987. I stopped by the apartment where Pam and the girls were living. They were gone. I was terrified. Where could they have gone?

I called the case worker, who was working with the situation. She told me to stay in touch with her, and if I heard from Pam, to let her know.

I was an emotional wreck. I was worried. Was she taking care of those two babies? Where could they be? Did they have something to eat? Were they warm and safe? Finally, three days later, Pam called.

"Where are you?" I shouted. "I'm a nervous wreck! I haven't been able to sleep, I can't eat! I've paced the floor, and shouted at God to please find my kid and my grandchildren!"

I heard her take a deep breath. "Mother," she said, "we are okay. We are in Washington, in a Women's shelter."

"Pam, you weren't supposed to leave Oregon!"

"Mother, just calm down. I've taken care of everything, and transferred the case."

"When are you coming home with those babies?"

"I will bring the children to your house on Thursday." She didn't say goodbye - there was just a dial tone. I was left with my feelings, wondering if she would show up.

I called Washington Children Services, and told them about the case. They sent out a case worker who tracked Pam down. They assured me Pam would be at my house on Thursday. I called the case worker in Oregon, and told her the latest developments. I was not to allow Pam to leave with the children. I was instructed to call the police if she insisted on leaving with them; the police had a number where they could get in touch with me directly.

Pam brought the children on Thursday. I called the case worker to let her know Pam had brought the children. While I was talking to her, she asked me if she could talk to Pam. She let her know there was a court hearing the following day.

I loved Pam. I knew it was my job to protect my grandchildren. I would do whatever it took to keep them safe. I didn't want to go to court, but I knew I had to. I wrestled with my thoughts and emotions that night. I tossed and turned. I walked the floor. I wrung my hands. I cried and asked God, "What could I have done differently? Did I say the wrong things to Pam?" God didn't answer, and I didn't have the answer.

Morning came too quickly. I couldn't eat. I drank a cup of coffee. I left to go to court. The dreaded hour, ten o'clock, came, and we were called into the court room. I was asked if Pam was a good Mother. I had to tell them she wasn't. I stood in the courtroom and wept.

Their dad was also under investigation because of his hot temper. I obtained custody until his name could be cleared. The court session was over, and Pam wanted to know why I told them she wasn't a good mother. "I had to tell them the truth; sometimes the truth is the most difficult item to reveal."

As I said those words, tears rolled down my cheeks. My body shook with emotion. My legs felt heavy, and my feet had lead in them. I slowly walked away. I quietly said, "I'm sorry, Pam."

We were lonely and sad without Grandma Wynn; it was difficult to be without her. We were thankful she didn't know how Pam was living her life in the drug world. The court ordered the children's dad to go to parenting classes, and he complied with the orders. Six months later, he obtained custody of his children.

We were helping their dad with the girls. Pam was nowhere to be found. I was working, and Wayne was retired. He was always good to lend a helping hand with the girls. They were two and three-years-old. They didn't ask about their mother, and I didn't have anything to tell them.

I was heavy-hearted, sad, worried, and wondering where she was. Many days, my eyes were red and puffy from crying. I tried my best to stay good-humored and pleasant. Wayne knew I was worried, and every once-in-awhile, he would put his arm around me, and quietly say in his gentle voice, "I'm here for you to lean on."

My dam of emotion would break, and I would weep. As he wrapped his arms around me, I would sob on his shoulder.

It was Saturday afternoon when the phone rang. I picked it up on the first ring. It was Pam. "Pam! Pam, where are you? Why has it taken so long for you to call? Are you all right?"

"Mother, calm down. I'm okay. I've married a man from India, and we're living in Houston, Texas. I'll keep in touch with you. How are my babies?"

I handed the phone to Wayne. I couldn't talk anymore. I stood and wept.

He told her about the children; she said she would call again. Life went on. The childrens' dad and I didn't seem to be on the same page. He wanted things done his way, and I had my own way of doing things. In his way of thinking, I should be doing things the way he wanted them done.

Pam seemed to be happy in Texas, and had a job. She talked about her husband. She seemed to be content and peaceful. I was hopeful one more time, maybe, she had found what she was looking for.

She called on a regular basis, to let us know how things were going for her. She missed her girls. She began to talk about moving back to Portland. She wanted to regain custody of her children. Her husband wanted to move to Seattle, because there were more job opportunities.

Pam called us a few months later, to let us know they were moving to Seattle. She said when they found a place to live, and when they were settled, they would come to Portland, so we could meet
her husband. We were excited about what was taking place. Pam also told us of her plans to go to a drug rehab center, because she knew she needed help with her drug addiction.

My hopes and dreams were wrapped up again. I knew I would help her in any way I could, to regain custody of her children. I felt like I was standing on the edge of insanity, wondering if all this was going to work for the good of everyone involved.

A few weeks later, Pam called. They were coming to Portland for the day, and could they come and have dinner with us? "Of course, you can! We're anxious and excited! We can hardly wait to meet him!" I replied.

They arrived about four in the afternoon. Pam introduced us to her husband. He was from India, tall and slender, olive skin, black hair, and chocolate brown eyes. He was pleasant, good humored, soft spoken, an easy person to be with.

We had roasted chicken, mashed potatoes, gravy, green salad that consisted of lettuce, tomatoes, cucumbers, radishes, red onion and grated carrots. We prepared peas with pearl onions. Good fresh coffee and ice cream for dessert. We talked and laughed all through dinner. Before we knew it, it was nine o'clock. Pam said to her husband, "We had better get going - we have to get to Seattle tonight."

He glanced at his watch. "Oh, my goodness! I guess we had better get on the road." He thanked us for a very pleasant evening, the good food, wonderful conversation, and assured us, "We will come back again." He shook Wayne's hand, and gave me a hug. Pam hugged and kissed us when she left.

It was a night I wanted to hang onto, along with the feelings I had deep inside: the feelings of hope that Pam would straighten her life out, and regain the custody of her children.

Pam called us a few weeks later to let us know she was in a drug rehab center. She invited us to come and see her. Labor Day weekend was approaching, and we decided we would go and see Pam at the rehab center. We were hopeful one more time. We were scheduled to have a group meeting at 2:00, on Saturday afternoon. We arrived at 1:30, and rang the doorbell - it was a locked-down facility. Pam came up the stairs with a sly grin on her lips.

I can still feel the anger I felt that day, so many years later. I knew this was some more lip service. Pam was good at knowing what to say and how to say it. It was learned from experience. Wayne and I sat like stone statues, as we listened to folks talk to their loved ones. My mind was set. My emotions were in a knot, my hands were sweaty, my mouth was as dry as a desert, and my heart was pounding. We loved her with all our hearts and souls.

I cleared my throat, looked at Pam, and I could feel the tears in my eyes. "Pam, this is the end of the line. This is where the bus stops. We will not return to another drug rehab center. We have been to the Morrison Center, Lutheran Family Services, White Shield Home for Girls, and AA. If you go out and use drugs again, you are on your own. We love you, but we want the best for you."

We rose to our feet, walked over to her, held her, kissed her, and we cried. It seemed like we were stuck to the floor - our feet couldn't move for a few seconds. "Pam, please call when you are finished with your program, and we will see where we go from here."

We walked to the door, turned, and waved to her as we left. Wayne held my hand as we walked to the car. I felt like I was watching a movie in slow motion. He wrapped his arms around me as we stood by the car; he quietly said, "Maybe she'll make it this time."

I tried to hold back the tears. My body shook, as I stood and sobbed in his arms. He gently lifted my chin, and said, "We will get through this together."

We got into the car to drive back to Portland. We were lost in our thoughts. My thoughts swirled in my mind. I was hopeful she would decide to change her behavior patterns. Scared she would give it lip service. What would I do about this or that? I kept silent. I knew I would have to wait and see what the outcome would be.

Wayne was quiet as usual - sometimes it was a blessing; this was one of those times. I could tell Wayne was doing some soul searching - the stern look on his face, the mist in his eyes, and the clearing of his throat. I reached over and patted him on the shoulder. "Are you okay?'

"Yes, just remember: where there's life there's hope."

As I rode in the car, my heart and mind were at war with each other. My heart said, "She'll make it," while my mind was saying, "What if she doesn't?"

The weeks went by; we stayed busy with the girls. We picked them up at Waverly Childrens' Home on Friday evening at six, and returned them on Sunday at four. Things were quiet. Pam hadn't called for several months. I felt a foreboding apprehension, a feeling of being abandoned by her.

It was a warm spring morning. The silence was broken by the ringing of the telephone. I picked up the receiver - it was Pam! My prayers had been answered! I was overwhelmed with emotion. My voice shook. "Pam! Pam! I'm so happy to hear from you! What has happened? We haven't heard from you for a long time!"

"Mother, slow down," she replied." I'm okay. I've graduated from the rehab program, found a job, left my husband, and filed for divorce."

"What in the world happened?" I asked. "We liked him. He seemed like a nice person, and I could tell he was in love with you."

"Mother, he IS a nice person - he's just not for me. Things weren't working out the way I wanted them to. I don't have time to tell you right now. I am going to move back to Portland. I'm going to hire a lawyer, find a job, get an apartment, and I'm going to regain custody of my girls. Listen, Mother, I haven't any more time to talk. I have to get to work, and I'm almost late. When I get moved to Portland, I'll tell you all about it. In the meantime, please don't worry. Everything will work out. Bye for now."

She was gone. I was left with a dial tone. The tears were running down my checks; my thoughts were swirling. I was hoping all her words would be true. She sounded so sure of herself. The feeling deep inside that I didn't want to address, was to be careful. It might not turn out the way you want it to. I decided I would think about it tomorrow.

  Pam showed up many months later. She rang the doorbell, walked into the house, as if she had just been here yesterday. She was excited. "Mom Dad! I found a job! And, I found an apartment a few blocks from here, but I need a co-signer. Will you co-sign for me?"

  Wayne and I looked at each other, nodded our heads up and down. "Of course, we will. We are excited for you, Pam. We are thankful you are home again."

  I was anxious, excited, and worried, all at the same time. I have heard many empty promises before, and wondered, deep inside of me, if this was another one of those times. Time would tell the real story.

  Pam went to work, taking care of her client; it was a live-in job, five-days-a week. Things seemed to be going along smoothly. She found a lawyer - his name was Howard. Pam wanted me to come with her to her first appointment. His office was in S.W. Portland. He reminded me of Columbo. He was a medium-sized man, dark brown hair, clear blue eyes. His office was a mess, piles of papers everywhere, and nothing seemed to be in order. He was smart, articulate, and knew exactly what he was talking about.

  He explained to Pam, "You have to stay clean and sober for at least six months, before you can get any visitation rights. For right now, I will get you visitations, supervised by your mother. Will this arrangement be okay with you, Sandra?"

  I nodded my head 'yes'.

  "And one more thing - you are not to bring any of your friends with you. The time you spend with your girls, is to be used to get reacquainted with them. Do you have any questions for me?"

  Pam shook her head no. She was allowed to come every other Saturday, from two until four.
I was so impressed with him, that I gave him a fifty-dollar check. I was confident Pam would really take responsibility for her life, and she would stay on the

straight and narrow path. She went to work, called me every day, letting me know she was okay. I was impressed, hopeful, engaged with the idea she was going to repair her life. From all outside appearances, it was going to be a reality.

She was coming to visit her girls at the appointed time. From the outside looking in, it appeared to be wonderful. They colored pictures, played games, baked cookies, and watched movies. We lived across the street from a school, and behind the school building was a small park. It contained swings, a merry-go-round, and a slide. Sometimes Pam and I would take the girls to the park.

It was a warm spring day, when Pam showed up with a male friend. I stepped over to her and whispered in her ear, "He's not allowed!" She said something to him, and he left. When she came into the living room, she sat down with the girls and seemed to be pre-occupied with her thoughts. All of a sudden, she said to me, "Can I take the girls to the park?" She knew I couldn't say no, and disappoint the girls.

I gave her a sharp stare. "For thirty minutes." I waited for ten minutes, then left and went to the park. There they were - Pam, the boyfriend, and the girls. I was livid, wild with rage and anger. I stepped over to the boyfriend. My voice shook as I looked at him with a firm stare said, "Get your ass out of here now! If I ever see you again, I'll strangle you to death!" He shrugged his shoulders as he walked away.

Pam stepped over to me. I said to her, "Nowhere on that piece of paper, does it say to bring your boyfriend with you."

She looked at me with a sly grin, as she said, "No one will ever know."

I firmly said, "The subject is closed." The girls had no idea what had taken place; they were busy playing on the swings and the merry-go-round. We went back to the house, had cookies and milk, then Pam kissed the girls and went home. I called Howard on Monday, to let him know what had taken place. His response was, "Her visitation rights are over."

Pam called on Friday, to tell me she was on a bus with her boyfriend, and they were going to Pennsylvania. I could feel the emotion in my body, the golf ball in my throat, tightness in my stomach, and tears that were forming in my eyes, as I said, "Pam, why are you going away? "What can I say or do to stop you?"

"You can't, Mother, you can't. The wild side of me is calling." She was gone. I was left with a dial tone. I wanted to stop her, but knew there was nothing I could do or say, to change the situation. Once again, I knew rules and regulations meant nothing to Pam. I wondered what I was going to tell the girls on Saturday, when they asked if their mother was coming to see them.

Friday evening came, and it was time to go and pick up the girls from Waverly Childrens' Home. As we rode along in the car, they wanted to know if their mama was going to come over. I told them we would talk about it when we got home.

When we arrived home, I took the girls into the bedroom, where we sat down on the bed. I could feel the lump that was forming, and cleared my throat. I could feel the tears in my eyes as I put my arms around them. "Girls, your mama has gone on a trip to Pennsylvania."

"Where is Pennsylvania?" they asked.

"Come on," I said," I'll show you where it is on the map. Oregon is right here, and Pennsylvania is way over here."

"Oh," they said, "that's a long way away."

"It sure is," I replied. They seemed to be okay - I was the one who wasn't okay. My emotions felt frozen. I could feel the tears, always close to the surface. I became aware I was sad. I was angry. I had been betrayed one more time. All my hopes and dreams that Pam would be a mother to her children, and take care of them, were gone in an instant. I was left to pick up the pieces one more time.

Wayne was showing signs of memory loss. He wasn't doing things he used to do. He quit cooking meals, driving the car, and he wouldn't talk on the phone. He would tell callers to talk to me, because he would get all mixed up.

I decided to take an extended vacation time in the summer. I knew inside of me, Wayne was not going to be with us for a long time. He was coming to the end of his life. I was going to spend as much quality time as possible with him. I loved him. He loved me. We fit together like gloves.

Every summer, from 1990-1996, I took six weeks off from my job; we went to visit relatives. Pam called every few weeks, and Wayne would always ask her when she was coming home. Pam would reply, "As soon as I get my stuff together."

It was November,1996. Wayne insisted I needed a different car. In his mind, he just knew my car was ready for the junkyard. I had a feeling he was trying to tell me he wasn't going to be here long, and he wanted to take care of things before he left. I knew we couldn't afford the car he was purchasing for me. It was important to him.

At that time, I decided I would take care of things at a later date.

While we were at the dealership, the sales lady's husband arrived. We were introduced to him - his name was Dan, who was a funeral director. I thought at the time, "This is odd. I don't need to know a person of this nature."

While we were talking about payments for the car, and the down payment, the sales lady gave me her business card. On the back, she had put her home phone number, and the number at the beauty salon where she worked part-time. She also put down her husband's phone number, and his pager number. Little did I know, that four months later, I would need those numbers.

March 26th,1997, is a date I will never forget. It was spring break for the girls. They always came to our house for the week. It was raining and cold, and they were tired of each other. Sarah wanted to go next door to play with her friends, and she wanted to go alone. I took Mary with me. It was my last client. I filled her medication box for the week. While I was there, I felt it was urgent for me to call home to see if things were okay.

Sarah answered the phone. She screamed, "Grandma! Grandma! It's my mother! She's dead! She's dead! My mother's dead!"

"Oh, my God, Sarah, I'll be right home!" I knew I had to keep my composure. I said goodbye to my client, and let her know I would see her next week.

As I drove the car towards home, Mary wanted to know what happened. I told her I couldn't talk about it in the car. We would share the news when we got home. I parked the car in the driveway in front of the garage, and as I stepped out of the car, my body felt like cement. My legs would barely move, and my feet were heavy.

We went into the house. Wayne and Sarah were weeping, with their arms around each other. In between sobs, Sarah said, "Grandma! Grandma! The police were here! My mother's dead!"

Wayne looked up, with tears streaming down his face. "They found her in a hotel room in Allen Town, Pennsylvania. It was a drug overdose. Here's the paper they gave to me. I don't know what to do with it."

I took the paper and slipped it into my pocket; we wrapped our arms around each and wept. I walked into the bedroom, shut the door, and called Dan at the funeral home, and explained what happened. I gave him the name of the funeral home in Pennsylvania, and the phone number. I was dazed, shocked! I was in a stupor. I went into the living room, and told Wayne I would handle the funeral arrangements.

Dan called me to let me know it would cost twenty-three hundred dollars, to bring Pam's body to Oregon. I made arrangements to have a meeting in the morning, and contacted the rest of the family members.

Twenty-three hundred dollars? Where are we going to find the money? God knew, I didn't. The following morning, the family met at the funeral home at ten o'clock. We wanted to know what twenty-three hundred dollars covered. Here's the list: The body must be embalmed, and placed in a pine box. A one-way ticket will be purchased. She will come from Allentown, Penn., to Portland, Oregon. She will be flown here in the baggage department.

The girls were with us, as I believed it was important for them to help pick out the cards we would hand out at the funeral service. I'm not sure I knew what I was doing, at the time. Maybe it was a nightmare, maybe I would wake up, and everything would be all right.

We gave Dan the money we had. The company I worked for took up a collection, along with the church we belonged to.

How could this be? I just talked to Pam a few weeks ago. I told her how much I loved her. Her dad wanted to know when she was coming home. The answer was the same: When I get my stuff together. Maybe her stuff was together, in the pine box she would arrive in. It wasn't the way I wanted it to be.

It was only the beginning of things to take place. We had to purchase a casket, money to transport her body to the cemetery, and the opening and closing of the gravesite.

I sat on my grandchild's bed. My hands covered my face - I sobbed, and my shoulders shook. Where, oh where, is the money going to come from? I heard a voice in my mind. It said to call John. I decided I must be hearing things. I called John's dad - he wasn't home. I talked to Rossi, John's brother. I told Rossi what happened, and he said he would have John call me; I was still part of the family. Wayne had worked for John and his family for almost fifty years.

John called later in the evening. I explained to him what happened. He said, "I'll bring a check for three-thousand dollars. This is my gift to you and your family. You and Wayne have always been there for me. You were there when I got married, you were there when my mother died, and you were there when my girlfriend was killed. I love you both."

The following day, we went to the funeral home to view Pam's body. It was eerie inside. I rang the bell that sat on the desk inside the door. We waited for someone to appear to give us instructions; it was deathly quiet. We heard the echo of Dan's footsteps, as he came down the hall. He knew who we were. He said, "Follow me, and I'll show you where she is located. Stay as long as you need to."

He opened the door, and we stepped into the room where she laid in the casket. I felt the lump in my throat, the tears rolling down my cheeks. I held onto the girls' hands, one on each side of me.

Mary looked up at me and said, "Can I touch my mother?" "Yes, I replied, "she will be cold." Mary touched her mother's arms. When she was finished, she took my hand. Sarah wanted to open her mother's eyes - she wanted to know what color her eyes were. I told her they were green, like mine.

The girls were ten and eleven. As I stood there, I knew a few years from now, they would mourn the mother they never knew. Pam was buried on the first of April,1997. A few days later, Wayne was diagnosed with Alzheimer and Parkinson diseases.

I wasn't surprised. For the last five-or-six-years, his behavior, and his ability to remember things, were becoming questionable. The things he used to do, he now did less and less. For example, he used to do a lot of cooking. He quit driving the car, wouldn't talk on the phone, and quit doing the laundry. He used to go for a walk, then quit going. He couldn't remember how to dim the lights on the car. He didn't know how to work the faucets in the bathroom, or how to take a shower.

It was July 20th, 1997. We were going to go to a church picnic. I knew I couldn't take him by myself. Our son, Sheldon, went with us. Wayne had been to this park before - today he didn't remember he had ever been there. He didn't know where the bathroom was, and couldn't figure out how to open the door. Sheldon became his escort. He took him to the facility, opened the door for him, and stayed outside until he was finished. It wasn't long until he was agitated and wanted to go home. Sheldon took him home.

The following morning, while we were still in bed, he looked at me and said, "Who are you?"

I said, "Who are you looking for?"

"I'm looking for Sandra."

"Does she look anything like me?"

He gave me a blank stare. "Well, I think so," he replied.

"Where did she go?"

"She went to Springfield, and I'm going to go and get my mother. We are going to go and get her, and bring her home."

I turned to him and said, "Well then, we had better get up and get dressed." While he was getting dressed, I took his car keys. I knew he was upside down in his mind, and his wires were coming apart. His mother had died in 1988 - ten years ago.

I fixed our breakfast, and we ate in silence. He didn't say anything more about going to find Sandra, and he didn't ask who I was. This was only the beginning of the events that were going to take place. A few nights later, he was standing at the foot of the bed, patting my leg.

"Wake up! Wake up! I've been lost!"

"Where have you been?"

"I was outside. Someone told me to go outside, because there were some kids out there who needed some toys. I went out there to give them some toys."

"At three o'clock in the morning?" I asked.

He decided he would go back to bed for a while. The following day, I had a friend of mine install an alarm system on the front and back door. There was an on-and-off switch. When the alarm went off, it was very loud.

I knew at this point, I had to keep track of him at all times. I began to feel like I was a warden, and Wayne was my prisoner. I was trapped; I couldn't let him out of my sight. He was entering the world of the lost, a world I couldn't enter, and I couldn't bring him back to my world. He would look at me with a blank stare, a flatness I can't describe.

He didn't know if he was in Minnesota, or Oregon. He saw horses across the street in a grassy field. He didn't know if they were riding horses, or work horses. He asked me if they were riding horses, and I told him that no, they weren't, because he didn't have any saddles. He seemed to be satisfied with the answer. He shrugged his shoulders and sat down in his chair, closed his eyes to rest. He often sat with his eyes closed. I would ask him if he was sleepy, and he would say no.

He never asked again who I was. I gave him showers, shaved him, and helped him get dressed. I was watching him crumble, in slow motion. I had no time to think about what was taking place. He saw people who weren't there, cats we didn't have, holes in the carpet, water that wasn't there. He saw a cat peeing in the closet; he couldn't get ready for bed. I closed the closet door so he couldn't see the cat we didn't have. He was okay then, and would let me get him ready for bed.

It was the middle of August, and Wayne was in a wheelchair; he was losing his ability to walk. By the end of the month, he lost control of his bladder. He was hospitalized, and by this time, he could no longer talk. He couldn't move his legs, or his arms. Everything had to be done for him. I knew this was the end of life for my darling husband.

September 5th, 1997, the doctor entered the room as I was shaving Wayne's whiskers. He glanced over at me and quietly said, "We need to talk about placing him."

I stopped him. "I know he's terminal. I'll take him home, and we will have hospice come with their services." I went on to tell him he had a hospital bed, a reclining wheelchair, and a Hoyer lift. "My family and friends will help me take care of him. This is the last loving item I can do for my darling."

The doctor stepped back from the bed. "I was wondering how I was going to tell you that he's terminal.

What kind of work do you do?"

"I work in home health - I'm a CNA."

"Okay," he replied, "I'll go get his discharge papers ready, and you can go home if you would like. I'll order an ambulance for him, and he will be taken home." I thanked him for his good service.

I called the family together, called my church friends, and explained to them that Wayne was coming home, and I would need them to help me. Family and friends came. They cooked and cleaned, helped me to turn him every two hours. We bathed him, fed him, and made sure he was warm, dry, and comfortable.

September 13th and 14th, I had a birthday party and open-house for Wayne. His sister and brothers, cousins, daughters, sons, grandchildren, and many friends, came to say goodbye to Wayne. I knew this was his last birthday.

I couldn't think about what I was going to do after he was gone. I couldn't think at all. I felt like this was a nightmare, and I would wake up, and everything would be okay again. I never spent a night alone. Someone always came to help me turn Wayne every two hours. They always slept on the couch and insisted I needed to sleep in my bed. My sleep was never restful, my body felt tense, like I was always listening for him to make some sort of sound.

Sunday, the 21st of September, sometime during the night, I dreamed this was the last night I would sleep in my bed. Wayne was going to leave this earth. I woke up in a cold sweat. I went out to the living room to see if he was all right. He was sleeping. I sat down at the table. I was scared, and my hands shook. Finally, I went back to bed, but I couldn't sleep.

The following morning, I noticed he was having trouble breathing. I called his doctor. He ordered some oxygen, which was brought to the house in a few hours. The nurse hooked up the oxygen, and immediately, he was breathing easier. Monday night, the 22nd of September, our son, Art, came to help with his dad. It was four a.m. This would be the fourth time we would turn him and wash his body. Wayne was turned toward me - I was holding Wayne's shoulder and hip. Art stepped back from the bed. "I can't do this anymore, Mother."

"Yes, you can," I replied. "Take a deep breath, and count to twenty"

He stepped toward the bed. "I'm okay now. I can finish."

After we were finished, and Wayne was sleeping, I looked at Art and knew this had been really a difficult one for him. I took a deep breath. "Art, you will never forget this night; you will probably never have another one like it. You and I will have a bond together, that we will not be able to explain, because there are no words to describe what we did together tonight."

"I know, Mother," he replied. He left for work, and I went to lie down in my bed. It was eight o'clock when I woke up. I was startled, and rushed out to the living room to check on Wayne; he was sleeping. It was past time to turn him. I was alone. I called my friend, Carlene. I asked her if she could come over and help me give Wayne a bed bath. She said, "Sure, I'll be right there."

After we had finished bathing him, and he was resting, I stepped into the bedroom to get the portable fan. I brought it out to the living room, plugged it in, and Wayne took his last breath.

I stood there. I couldn't move. I stared. I waited.

He never took another breath. I watched as the color left his body. I called hospice, and they came and gave him another bath. The coroner came – remember, you are not dead until he says you are.

I called the family, and they came to say goodbye. Tyanna, was the youngest grandchild - she was five. She walked up and down the bedroom. She looked her Grandpa up and down. She looked at me, and said, "Where are his hands, Grandma?"

"They are under the sheet." I replied. I placed his hands on top of the sheet. Tyanna felt his arms and hands. She looked at me and said, "You know, he is really dead."

Her brother, Logan, was six. He looked at his

Grandpa, went over and sat down on the couch beside the pastor. He said, "You know, my Grandpa made the best peanut butter and jelly sandwiches! I'm really going to miss those sandwiches."

The folks from the funeral home came to get his body; my friends Don and Nina, were there with me. I stepped over to the two young men. I said, "Do you mind if we help you load him on the gurney? He's a large man, and this is the last loving item I can do for my darling. I know that you know what you are doing, however, if you were to bang his head, that would be the last thing I would remember."

They were so kind and gentle. "Of course, you may help us."

We got him on the gurney with one gentle lift. I bent down and kissed him on his lips. "I love you, my darling." He was gone. I stood and stared at the empty bed. How could this be? He took care of us. He was gentle and kind, he loved us and we loved him, and now he's gone. The room was as quiet as a tomb. Time itself seemed to stand still.

Nothing had changed outside. People were still going shopping, going to work, or school. The sun was still shinning, and very few people knew what had just taken place. I had just lost a part of myself. I felt disconnected to everything and everyone.

The funeral came and went - Wayne and Pam are buried side by side. I had to begin a new chapter in my life. I had no idea how it was going to happen. I didn't know if I could continue to be a caregiver.

I decided I would learn to drive a Tri Met Lift Bus. I applied for the job and signed up to take their training. The first day, I learned about abrasions, bubbles, and cuts on tires. How to check the oil, and the bus ran on fuel, not gas - it was called fuel. We were to check the bus every morning. That meant to check the oil, tires, walk around the bus, and check for dents. Plus, I had to learn to back this bus up into the garage.

While I was on the bus with the instructor and rest

of the students, we would go through different neighborhoods, and parts of the city. I started missing the folks I used to take care of. I would think: I used to have clients in this neighborhood, or in this part of the city. I decided I may not like this kind of job.

After a stressful day on the bus, we were listening to the radio calls; someone was lost, and they couldn't find the hospital entrance where they were supposed to pick up a passenger. I went home that evening, knowing I didn't want to drive a bus. I went to bed that night, tossed and turned, walked the floor, and wondered what I was going to say to the supervisor in the morning.

My daughter, Cheryl, was staying with me at the time. She moved back to Portland, from Bishop, California. She looked at me as she said, "Mother, what is wrong with you today? You look awful!"

"Cheryl, I don't want this job. I want to take care of the clients I used to take care of."

"Well," she replied, "go in and tell your boss you don't want to drive a bus."

I left and went to work. I went to the supervisor's office. His door was open, and I walked into the room. He looked up from his paperwork, pushed his glasses up that were almost to the end of his nose, and cleared his throat, "Can I help you with something?"

"Yes, you can," I replied, "I don't want to drive a lift bus."

"Well, what do you want to do?"

"I want to take care of the terminally ill."

"Then, that's what you need to do. Go and do it with my blessings. I appreciate it when folks like you come and tell me early on, instead of waiting six months to tell me, that they don't want to drive the bus."

I thanked him, and went home and called my former boss. I asked her if I could have my job back. She replied with, "Yes, come to my office in the morning, at 9:00."

The following morning, I walked into her office. She handed me my schedule for the day. I was thankful and grateful that my boss was willing to give my job back to me. I stood in her office, and could feel the tears that were close to the surface. I had a lump in my throat as big as a potato. She wrapped her arms around me, and quietly whispered, "I'm glad you're back with us.

I wiped my tears, and took a deep breath. "I had to come back. This is work of the soul. This is life in the trenches. This is where the rubber meets the road."

She stepped back from me, and looked into my eyes, "Yes, Sandra, you are one of a kind."

I felt as light as a feather. I knew at that moment, this is where I belong.

My first client lived in S.W. Portland, on the fifth floor of an apartment building. Florence was eighty-five-years-old, soft white hair as soft as cotton. She was about four-feet-eleven inches tall, and probably didn't weigh ninety pounds soaking wet. She had beautiful soft brown eyes, the color of dark chocolate. Her one-bedroom apartment was always neat and tidy. Nothing was out of place.

I rapped on her door, just like I used to, and she answered, "Come in, Sandra."

I walked in and asked her, "How did you know it was me?"

"The office called yesterday, and your boss told me you would be here today. I'm so glad you're back. I was sad when you were gone."

"Did they take good care of you?" I wanted to know.

"Well, yes, but it just wasn't the same way you take care of me." She walked over to the couch, laid down, and folded her arms across her chest. I knew it was my cue for our routine.

I sat down in the chair next to the couch. Her eyes were closed. "How are you today, Florence?"

"I'm dying."

I put my hand on her forehead, looked her over. "Not today."

"Why not?"

"Color's too good."
"What color do I have to be?"
"Pasty white."
"Okay, then I'll take a shower."

Into the bathroom we went. I never washed her hair; she always had it done at the beauty shop. I washed her back, legs, and feet. The rest of her parts were hers. I closed the curtain so she would have some privacy. I helped her dry her body, and get dressed. We went out to the living room. She took my hand in hers, and took a deep breath. She quietly said, "Please don't leave me again."

I put my arms around her. "I promise I will stay; this is where I belong." We were both teary eyed when I left. She also knew I would be back in a couple. of days.

My life was different now. I didn't know how I was going to make a new life for myself. I began to ask my clients questions about how they felt when their husbands died. The answers I received were profound, penetrating, and wise. Their eyes would fill with tears. I can still hear their answers: 'I felt like I had lost half of myself.' 'I couldn't think.' 'I didn't want to go on without him.' 'I wanted to die. I couldn't, there was nothing else to do, I had to go on living'.

I began to realize I was okay. This is what happens when you lose your mate. I wondered about myself, when I would go to the grocery store, and didn't know what I was doing there. I would forget why I was there, so I would go back home again. I felt disconnected. I would cry at odd times. If I saw someone driving a piece of heavy equipment, I would cry. Or a heavy feeling of sadness, and I would be weeping.

Christmas was approaching. I had no interest, and couldn't focus. My mind was someplace else. My daughter, Cheryl, bought the Christmas tree, decorated it, did the shopping, sent Christmas cards, and cooked dinner. What I would have done if she had not been there? I have no answer.

I began to heal at a slow rate. The girls and I went

to the Doughy Center once a week. They have support groups for folks who have lost family members. The girls and I were in the same situation. They lost their mother and their grandfather, within six months; I lost my husband and my daughter. I learned I was not alone. There would be days that would be smooth, other days would be rocky and hard. I would have to take one small step at a time. We were at the Doughy Center for six months.

19

The girls were troubled - the situation with their dad was not stable. He was hot tempered, and had no patience with the them. He would have a temper tantrum, and the girls would call the police. The police would call me, and I would bring them to my house for the weekend. They were unhappy with dad, and wanted to stay with me. I obtained custody of them in 1998.

They were troubled, and I didn't have the tools to fix them. They had no freedom at Dad's house, but they had some freedom at my house. It was too much for them - they simply decided to do what they pleased. They wouldn't go to school, wouldn't obey any rules, stayed out late, and had temper tantrums. Their behavior was out of control. Many times, I had to call the police because their behavior was uncontrollable.

I kept a journal of their behavior, and finally had to file a petition to place them in foster care. I truly believed I could make a difference in their lives. I had taken on a bigger job that I wasn't qualified to do. I didn't have the right tools.

I stood in the courtroom, and explained to the judge how I wasn't physically or emotionally able to care for the girls. Their behavior was out of control. I felt like I was inside out. The tears rolled down my cheeks, my hands shook, my voice was shaky, and my legs felt like water. The judge quietly said, "They will be placed in foster care."

I looked up at the judge with tears in my eyes. I said, "Thank you." I left the courtroom and went home. My insides felt heavy and sad. Both the girls were placed in the same foster home. The situation at the foster home unraveled my youngest granddaughter. Mary made the decision to run away with a friend of hers. The State Patrol picked them up in California. My granddaughter was returned to Oregon, and placed in a locked-down facility in S.E. Portland.

By this time, I had to face the reality that I couldn't

pay my bills. Wayne's income was gone, the money I had in a trust fund was gone, and the money I received from his life insurance was slowly being spent. The only income I received, was from my job and a small pension. I couldn't pay for the car Wayne insisted we needed to buy. The Master Card was charged to the max. There was only one thing left to do: file bankruptcy. I knew the world wouldn't stop turning, and I was out of options. I called my good lawyer, Walter, and made an appointment to see him the following week.

Walter was the kind of lawyer I could talk to, as if he were my next-door neighbor. We were making chit-chat over a cup of coffee. He leaned back in his chair that was behind his desk, folded his hands on his stomach, his eyes were kind and gentle as he said, "Sandra, you have had a difficult year. Your daughter and your husband died within six months of each other. Wayne's income is gone, and I don't suppose you make a bundle of money. If by chance, or by some kind of good luck you have some money, I don't want to know about it. All I need to know is, do you have enough money to file for bankruptcy?"

I cleared my throat, and let out a big sigh. I felt like I was shuffling my thoughts. "Walter, I have enough money to file the papers, and I need another car. I hope you know someone who sells cars at a lower price than the used car lot." I wasn't going to cry, but all of a sudden, my throat tightened. Tears slid down my cheeks.

Walter walked over and sat down beside me, handed me a Kleenex. "Sandra, I have a friend who sells cars at a low price. I know you can buy one for a thousand dollars. What kind of a car do you want?"

"Just a simple car with an automatic transmission."

"Okay," he replied, "I'll call you in a few days, and let you know about a different car."

I felt like a ten-pound-weight had been lifted from my shoulders. I feel better when I have a plan to work with. Walter called me a few days later, to let me know his friend had a car for me. He gave me his name and phone number. I called him and made arrangements to go pick up the car.

Life went - on the dealership sent a man out to repossess the Dodge I couldn't pay for, and I continued going to work. I had an old car - it would get me from point A to point B.

My troubles were not over. The manager of the duplexes where I lived, came to visit me one day; it wasn't a social call. He had come to tell me I had thirty days to move. He had received numerous complaints against me because of the numerous times the police had been to my house. "A complaint will not be filed against you, so it won't be on your record when you find a new place to live. I'll give you a good report." I told him I understood his position, and I thanked him for his kindness.

I was almost panic stricken. What was I going to do? Where was I going to find a place to live? "Well," I said to myself, "you had better start thinking. I'll call my friend, Mary." I placed the call to my friend, Mary, who said there was an apartment for rent next to her. I moved to Gresham. I had no idea when I moved, I would be living in the same neighborhood as my granddaughter.

It was a Sunday afternoon, quiet, a day I felt like I was the only person on the planet. I was shopping at Fred Myer's, standing in the middle of the aisle, looking at some items. I looked up to see Sarah in front of me, with tears in her eyes. "Grandma, I want to come home."

I was frozen like a statue. I couldn't talk. I felt tears roll down my cheeks. There was a lump in my throat, and I couldn't speak. I could feel my insides turning to jelly. I took a deep breath. I shook my head from side to side. I quietly said, "With all of my heart, I wish I could." I slowly turned and walked away.

I knew I had to find a counselor. I had to talk about it. I knew my mind was set like cement. My heart was like jelly, and I had to find a way to be in-between jelly and cement. I went to see a Mental Health Counselor; I wrestled with my decision for several weeks, before I could put the situation into words, and make a decision I could live with. It was one more time when I would be standing between a rock and a hard place. I would be inside out again.

It was a cool October morning, gray sky, and it felt like it could rain at any moment. I felt alone, misunderstood, scared, and most of all, I felt like I had failed. I knew the decision I had to make. I also knew it was tearing me apart on the inside.

I parked the car, got out, locked the door, and went upstairs to my appointment. I could feel my insides shaking, my heart was pounding, and my mouth was dry. I cleared my throat and began my speech. The tears rolled down my cheeks.

I love my Mary and Sarah. I have done all I can do for them at this time. I have struggled with them, and for them, since they have come into this world. I have their best interest in my heart. It would be a disaster if I took them back home with me. It is clear to me I have to do what is best for them and for me. I love them dearly, and I will stay in their lives. My heart knew this was the decision I had to make. I sat and wept. I didn't know I had so many tears.

The counselor walked over to me, and put his arms around me. He quietly said, "You will be okay. It was a heavy decision to make."

I knew I would be okay. I also knew it would take time. I wanted the girls to be okay with the decision I had to make. I needed time for me to become strong enough to explain to the girls, why I had to make the decision for them to stay in foster care. All of us needed healing time.

It took some time for me to understand they had some lessons to learn, and they wouldn't be able to learn them if they were home with me. I had to give them their freedom, and allow them to grow as adults. I didn't want them to learn their lessons the hard way. I wanted to protect them. I wanted to hold them close, as I once did when they were babies. I had some more hard lessons I had to learn.

They are in their thirties now, and I learned, and I am still learning. I don't have to approve of everything they do. I just need to love them, and not give them a lecture, just try to understand where they are.

As I look back over the events of my life, I have come to understand that we don't have any control over when we were born, the kind of parents we had, or the things that took place when we were children. I have a choice about my attitude, and the way I live my life today.

I'm thankful for the parents I had. They shaped my character, gave me the inner strength I didn't know I had. I learned early on, about the hard knocks in life.

The man I married when I was sixteen, was twenty-one. We had no idea we would almost destroy each other. We came from abusive places. We were acting out what we had been taught. I knew about love and kindness, when I didn't know of it. There is a world of difference. I knew how to respond to abusive behavior - I had lots of experience.

I learned of love and kindness when I married Wayne. He was a quiet man who spoke volumes by the way he lived. He was forty-four and I was twenty-six. He was in the prime of his life, and was willing to care for three young children. He went to work every day; he was a man of his word. I didn't know what to do with a man who meant what he said. I was scared and waiting for the day we would have an argument, and he would be out the door. It never came. He went to work. He came home.

Wayne showed me what love and kindness was. He lived it. He kissed me every morning and told me he loved me. He did the same every night. We had two boys together. When the grandkids came along, he helped with them. He loved all the children like his own.

About the author

I live in a retirement community. I have five grown children, seven grandchildren and three great grandchildren.

Sandra Wynn

Made in the USA
San Bernardino, CA
22 July 2019